LOVE MUM

Love mum

Tina Maree

Contents

Love Mum! The Aussie Mum Series

Written by:
Tina Maree

Copyright

Printed and Bound by:
Lighting source Australia
Part of the IngramSpark Group
www.ingramspark.com
Printed in Australia
First Printing Edition, 2024
ISBN 978-0-9756351-0-0

Love Mum

LOVE MUM, BECAUSE YOU CANT LIVE ON TEARS AND TOAST!

In Dedication of my children

In Dedication of My Children, Isabella and Nicholas

To my greatest creations (yes, even better than my cleaning hacks and slow cooker recipes that you both *love* sooooo much): Isabella and Nicholas.

Isabella, my little tornado of creativity, sass, and downright determination—you've shown me that no problem is too big for a dramatic sigh, a full-blown crying fit, and a nap. When you set your mind to something, absolutely nothing (and no one) is going to stand in your way. You've made me proud in ways I could never put into words. And although there were times I thought you might be the very death of me, the constant fight over 2 day old bread your complete lack of understanding that fruit and vegetables are not perfect and if they are they possibly are not the fruit and vegetables you want to be eating!! we made it through—stronger, wiser, and well still living.

Nicholas, my human encyclopedia of curiosity—you who give me one-word answers all day and then, just as I'm about to turn off my lamp for the night, launch into an hour-long story or ask questions that would stump a physicist. You've mastered the art of wandering to the kitchen at *just* the right time to hear the tea your sister is about to spill. You've taught me that life is best lived with wide-eyed wonder and just the right amount of chaos.

You've both been my toughest critics and my quietest cheerleaders, constantly reminding me that I'm not as cool as I like to think—but you love me anyway I think. This book wouldn't exist without the countless lessons you've taught me about patience, resilience, and the fine art of picking my battles (especially when it comes to whose used all the hot water).

Thank you for being my inspiration, and the reason I keep showing up—through burnt taco shell, messy houses which apparently are not messy, and the ever-present chaos of running late (again). Love you more than Raffaellos,

Love Always and forever Mum

1

Welcome to the Kitchen

Welcome To The Kitchen

Welcome to the jungle—aka your kitchen. No more GOOGLING, "How do you know when sausages are cooked?" You've got this. Armed with a few gadgets, some basic recipes, and a truckload of "love mum" spirit, you'll be cranking out meals that are not just edible but downright impressive. Or, at least, not burnt to a crisp. Start small, stay calm, and remember—cereal is always a fallback option.

Your Kitchen Starter Pack

Essential Tools

Here's what every kitchen needs to get the job done:

- **Knife (A Decent One)**: Not the butter knife you've been using to cut carrots. And ideally One that can slice a tomato without mashing it into soup.
- **Cutting Board**: To save your bench tops from looking like a crime scene.....
- **Frying Pan**: The MVP of the kitchen. Use it for everything from eggs to stir-fry.
- **Saucepan**: Perfect for boiling pasta, rice, or water for your tea when the kettle dies.
- **Wooden Spoon**: Durable, reliable, and excellent for threatening anyone who steals your food.
- **Baking Tray**: Essential for roasting veggies, baking cookies, or creating sweet potato fries.

Game-Changing Appliances

You don't need them all, but these gadgets will take you from "meh" to "master chef":

- **Toaster**: Not just for bread—think crumpets, raisin toast, or reheating leftover pizza.
- **Kettle**: Your best mate for instant noodles, tea, and speeding up boiling water.

- **Microwave**: Great for reheating, defrosting, and creating dessert in a mug.
- **Blender**: For smoothies, soups, or emergency margaritas.
- **Pie Maker**: The Kmart legend. It's not just for pies—try poached eggs, mushrooms, pancakes, or mini quiches.
- **Rice Cooker**: The "set it and forget it" genius for perfect rice every time.
- **Cupcake Maker**: Not just for cupcakes; make pancakes, omelettes, or mini frittatas.
- **Slow Cooker**: Chuck everything in, walk away, and return to a meal that makes you look like you've been slaving away all day.
- **Sandwich Press**: The ultimate multi-tasker—perfect for toasties, flatbreads, reheating pizza, or grilling just about anything.

Quick and Easy Recipes (That Don't Suck)

"Too Easy" Breakfast Burrito"

You will need

- 2 eggs
- 1 wrap (yes, the Woolies ones are fine)
- Cheese, tomato, spinach, or whatever is in the fridge.

How to Do It:

- Beat eggs like you're mad at them. Scramble in a pan on a low to medium heat refer to "how to know when cooked section"of book.
- Throw eggs and toppings into a wrap, fold it up, and devour.

One Pot Italian Chicken Pasta

You'll Need:

- chicken thighs can use left over BBQ chicken
- Spiral Pasta
- Liquid Stock chicken
- Sun dried tomato pesto
- Thickend Cream
- Oil
- cheese grated

How to Do It:

- Heat the oil in a large deep fry pan over a high heat cook chicken for approximately five minutes or until ground all over occasionally unless you're using barbecue chicken then just slightly heat this through

- Stir in pasta, Stock 3/4 of a cup, pesto and 1/2 cup of water then bring to a simmer.
- Reduce heat to medium cover pan and simmer during occasionally for 12 to 15 minutes until pasta is cooked
- Add a 1/3 cup cream to the pan and cook stirring for one minute or until heated through then Serve pasta topped with remaining pesto. Drizzle with remaining cream and sprinkle with cheese if desired.

Pie Maker Poached Eggs & Mushrooms

You'll Need:

- Eggs
- mushrooms
- butter
- water.

How to Do It:

- Crack an egg into one pie maker compartment, add water.
- Add mushrooms with butter into another compartment.
- Close the lid. Poached perfection.

Lazy Fried Rice

You'll Need*:*

- Leftover rice
- frozen veggies
- soy sauce
- 1 egg
- oil

How to Do It*:*

- Scramble the egg in a pan on a low medium heat once cooked removed Referred to "how do I know when it's cooked" section of the book.
- Fry rice and veggies, add soy sauce, on a low medium heat and mix in the egg.

One-Pot Spaghetti

You'll Need*:*

- Spaghetti
- canned tomatoes
- garlic jar is fine
- veggies

How to Do It*:*

- Boil a pot of water on high once bubbling add the pasta cook, (refer to section "how to know if its cooked" section once cooked drain

- Add the rest of the ingredients to the pot turn down to a low heat cook for around 10 min add past and cook it all together.
- Add cheese. You're officially fancy.

Chocolate Mug Cake

You'll Need:

- 4 tbsp self-raising flour
- 2 tbsp cocoa powder
- 3 tbsp sugar
- 3 tbsp milk

How to Do It:

- Mix in a mug. Microwave for 90 seconds. Instant dessert!

Eay Cheesy 2 minute noodles

You'll Need:

- Olive oil
- Butter
- One brown onion, finely chopped
- 1 tablespoon of plain flour
- Four middle bacon rashes trimmed roughly chopped
- Four packets of Maggie two minute noodles chicken flour
- 2 cups of milk
- 1 cup of frozen peas
- 1 cup of grated tasty cheese

How to Do It*:*

- Heat oil and butter in a large deep frying pan over medium heat add onion and bacon cook stirring occasionally for five minutes or until onions are soften transferred 2 tablespoons of onion mixture to a small bowl covered to keep warm.
- Add flour and two of the chicken flavoured sachets from noodles, discard remaining flavoured sachets, cook stirring for one minute reduce heat to medium gradually steering milk and 2 cups of water. Bring to a simmer. A Sim is just below boiling. Add noodles cook sterling occasionally to break up noodles for two minutes or until noodles tender.
- Add peas and cheese cook for further one to 2 minutes until your peas a bright green and tender season with Saltand pepper toss to combine
- Remove noodles from heat sprinkle with onion mixture and Serve

Sausage and Veggie Bake

You'll Need*:*

- Sausages,
- potatoes,
- carrots,
- zucchini,
- olive oil,
- salt, and pepper.

How to Do It:

- Chop veggies roughly, toss with oil, salt, and pepper.
- Bake with sausages in a baking dish at 200°C for 30 minutes or until the sausages are cooked and a fork can easy go into the pototoes (refer to how to know when its cooked section of the book.).

Slow Cooker Pulled Chicken

You'll Need:

- 4 Chicken breasts,
- 1 cup of BBQ sauce.
- 1/2 chicken stock or water
- One small onion, finely chopped
- Two cloves of garlic, minced or 2 teaspoons from a jar
- 1 tablespoon of brown sugar
- Salt pepper for taste

How to Do It:

- Place everything in the slow cooker at the chicken, barbecue sauce, chicken stock, onion, garlic, brown sugar, salt, and pepper to your slow cooker. Give it a quick mix to cook the chicken.
- Cook either on low for 6 to 7 hours or high for 3 to 4 hours until chicken is tender and easily shredded with a fork
- Serve on burger buns, and wraps, over rice, or nachos, or stuffed in baked potatoes at coleslaw for extra crunch
- **Extra;** Add a splash of apple cider vinegar or a dash of hot sauce if you'd like a tangy cake

- **Extra;** Double the barbecue sauce if you want it to be extra saucy
- This is also can go in the freezer

Fancy Rice Cooker Risotto

You'll Need:

- 1 1/2 cup Arborio rice,
- 1 tablespoon of olive oil or butter
- One small onion finally chop
- Two garlic clove, minced or 2 teaspoons of garlic from a jar
- One cup of sliced mushrooms
- 4 cups of chicken or vegetable stock
- 1/2 of grated Parmesan cheese
- 2 tablespoons of cream
- Salt and pepper to taste

How to Do It:

- In a pan add oil butter then cook the onion and garlic into soft toss in the mushrooms and cook until they begin to soften and smell amazing
- Add rice to the pan and cook for a minute to cook the grains at half a cup of Stock and stir until it's mostly absorbed
- Transfer to rice cooker add the rest of the Stock give everything a stir and close the lid set the rice cooker to white rice or regular cook depending on your model
- Let it work it's magic. It'll take about 25 to 30 minutes halfway through, give it a quick stir if your cooker allows. If not don't stress.

- When it's done, stirring Palmerson, cream, and a bit more stock or hot water if it is needed to loosen it up seasoned to taste
- Serve it on a plate with an extra cheese cracked pepper and maybe a little bit of a drizzle of some nice oil

Banana Bread for People Who Can't Be Bothered
(3 Ingredients. No Excuses.)

You'll need:

- 2 sad, overripe bananas (the blacker, the better – they're practically begging to be bread)
- 2 cups self-raising flour (the magic flour that *lifts* itself. Genius.)
- 1 can of *Top Caramel Condensed Milk* (the fancy Nestlé one in the gold tin – you're basically a chef already).

How to do it:

Mash the Bananas:

- Chuck those bananas into a bowl and mash them like they owe you money.
- It's fine if there are a few lumps—nobody's judging your mashing technique.

Mix It All Together:

- Add the self-raising flour and the can of caramel condensed milk to the bowl.
- Stir until everything's combined and looks like thick, gooey batter. Don't overthink it.

Prep Your Tin:

- Line a small bread tin with baking paper (or just grease it if you're living dangerously).
- Pour the mixture into the tin and spread it out evenly.

Bake It:

- Shove the tin into the oven at 180°C (350°F). Bake until a skewer comes out clean—about 40-50 minutes.
- **Pro Tip:** If you don't have a skewer, use a butter knife. If it comes out gloopy, keep baking.

Eat and Brag:

- Let it cool *a bit* (or burn your fingers because patience is hard).
- Slice it up, slap on some butter if you're feeling fancy, and enjoy!

Bonus Tip: This bread is so easy, you'll be making it every week. Your friends will think you're a baking wizard. **Love, Mum**

How to Know When It's Cooked?

(Without Calling Mum and saying can I eat this?)

Chicken
How to Check:

- Cut into the thickest part—there should be no pink meat or juices.
- If you've got a thermometer, chicken should be 75°C inside. (If you don't have one, they're like $10—worth it!)
- No thermometer? Push down with a fork. If the juices run clear, you're good to go.

Sausages
How to Check:

- Slice one open—it should be cooked all the way through with no raw or pink bits.
- The outside should be golden and slightly crispy, but not burnt.
- If it smells amazing and sizzles when you poke it, chances are you're on the right track.

Pasta
How to Check:

- Grab a piece and taste it! It should be soft but still a bit firm (this is called *al dente*, which is Italian for "fancy but not mushy").
- If it feels like chewing rubber, it needs more time. If it's dissolving in your mouth, you've gone too far—but hey, sauce can save anything.

Rice
How to Check:
Take a bite—it should be soft but not gluey.

- If it's crunchy, add a tiny bit more water and cook for another few minutes.

Eggs
How to Check:

- **Fried Eggs**: The whites should be fully set (not jiggly), and the yolk should look glossy.
- **Scrambled Eggs**: When they look creamy but not runny, they're ready.
- **Poached Eggs**: The whites should hug the yolk like a cosy jumper. If it's all wobbly, give it another minute.

Vegetables
How to Check:

- For boiled or steamed veggies: stab them with a fork. If it slides in easily, they're done.
- For roasted veggies: they should be slightly crispy on the outside and soft inside.
-

Confidence-Boosting Tips for Beginner Cooks

1. **Don't Rush It**: Cooking takes time. Start with low or medium heat to avoid burning things before they're cooked.
2. **Taste as You Go**: If it tastes good halfway through, you're doing fine. If it doesn't, add salt, spice, or cheese.
3. **Timer Hack**: Use your phone to set timers for everything—burnt food is just food that forgot it had a timer.
4. **Embrace Mistakes**: Everyone overcooks pasta or under-seasons their soup at first. Laugh it off and try again.
5. **Batch Cook Like a Pro**: Make extra, freeze portions, and thank yourself later.

Why You've Got This

Cooking is just assembling stuff and heating it up. Start small, practice, and don't be afraid to mess up you are already ahead of the game just by trying.

Now go fry something, you got this!

LOVE MUM

IS IT COOKED YET?

CHICKEN
Depends on preference

No pink, juices run clear
Internal temp: 75°C

BEEF
Rare ▶ Well done

Slightly pink is okay
Internal temp: 70°C

PORK
Slighty pink is okay

Flakes easily, opaque

Tender but not mushy

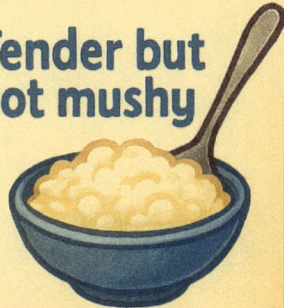

EGGS
No runny whites
(unless soft-boiled)

Love Mum

2

Cleaning Hacks You'll Thank Yourself For Later

Why Cleaning Doesn't Suck (That Much)

Cleaning might not sound thrilling, but it's the ultimate glow-up for your space. With a few clever tricks, some cheap supplies, and a good dose of Aussie ingenuity, you'll have a clean, fresh-smelling home that says, "I've got this adulting thing sorted" even if you haven't.

Your Cleaning Arsenal

Here's your go-to toolkit for tackling dirt, grime, and the occasional "What is THAT?" moment:

- **Vinegar**: The Swiss Army knife of cleaning supplies. Cheap, effective, and smells like fish and chips (temporarily).
- **Bicarb Soda**: A miracle powder for scrubbing, deodorising, and looking like you know what you're doing.
- **Dish Soap**: Not just for dishes—great for windows, sneakers, and even your sink drama.
- **Microfibre Cloths**: The dust and dirt magnets of the cleaning world.
- **Spray Bottle**: Essential for DIY cleaning solutions (or pranking housemates).
- **A Broom, Mop, and Bucket**: For those "the floor is lava" situations.
- **Vacuum Cleaner**: Preferably lightweight, so it doesn't feel like an arm workout.
- **Fragrance Oil**: The secret to a home that smells expensive, even on a budget.
- **Garbage Bags**: For trash, decluttering, or stashing junk when someone "pops by."
- **Old Socks**: The Aussie dusting hack we don't talk about enough.

DIY Hacks for That Luxe "I Cleaned" Vibe

Signature Scent Spray

You'll Need:

- A spray bottle
- Water
- 6 drops of fragrance oil (those cheap ones they use in candles are perfect).

How to Do It:

- Fill the spray bottle with water, add the fragrance oil, and shake it like a Polaroid picture.
- Spray on lounge cushions, curtains, or anywhere you want to smell fancy.

Fragrance Oil Diffuser

- Grab a cheap oil diffuser (Kmart or The Reject Shop sell them for under $15).
- Add a few drops of fragrance oil with water, and your room will smell amazing in no time.

The Vinegar and Water Cleaning Revolution

Let's hear it for vinegar, the underrated hero of the cleaning world. Here's how to use it (and a bit of water) to clean just about everything:

Shower Glass

- Mix equal parts vinegar and water in a spray bottle.
- Spray onto the glass, leave for 5 minutes, then wipe with a cloth or sponge.
- Rinse with water and pat dry with a microfibre cloth for a streak-free finish.

Windows That Don't Look Like Frosted Glass

- Spray vinegar and water on the glass. Wipe with newspaper (yes, really it's magic).
- Streak-free windows that even your nosy neighbours will envy.

Timber Floors

- Add half a cup of vinegar to a bucket of warm water. Mop floors gently (not too wet imber doesn't like baths).
- Result: shiny floors without the toxic chemical smell.

Kitchen Counters and Tables

- Spray with vinegar and water. Wipe clean with a cloth.
- Bonus: vinegar is food-safe, so it's perfect for the kitchen.

Mirrors

- Spray vinegar and water, wipe with a lint-free cloth or paper towel.
- Boom no more toothpaste splatter staring back at you.

Fridge Freshener

- Use vinegar and water to wipe shelves and drawers.
- Kills germs and gets rid of that "mystery smell."

Tile Grime

- Mix vinegar and water, spray on grout, and scrub with an old toothbrush.
- Clean tiles, zero elbow grease.

Pet Accidents

- For cleaning up after furry friends, vinegar neutralises smells and disinfects.

Everyday Cleaning Hacks

The "Panic Clean"

Someone's at the door, and your house looks like a cyclone hit?

- Dump clutter into a laundry basket and shove it somewhere no one will look.
- Wipe surfaces with a damp cloth.
- Spray your new signature scent (look at you, so fancy).

The Sock Trick

For lazy dusting.

- Slip a sock on your hand and run it over blinds, fans, or shelves.
- Bonus: it doubles as a weird puppet for cleaning motivation.

BBQ Cleaning Made Easy

- Rub half an onion over a hot grill. Degreases and smells like backyard brilliance.

Decluttering Without Tears

- Haven't used it in a year? Chuck it. Unless it's a Bunnings sausage sizzle apron.... those are sacred.

Room-by-Room Cleaning Cheats
Bedroom

- **Quick Fix**: Make your bed. Seriously, it makes the whole room look 100x better.
- **Weekly**: Dust surfaces, vacuum, and chuck dirty clothes in the laundry.

Kitchen

- **Quick Fix**: Wipe benches, stack dishes (or shove them in the dishwasher).

Weekly:

- Clean the stovetop with bicarb and vinegar.
- Wipe out the fridge, get rid of science experiments.
- Take the bins out before they reach toxic levels.

Bathroom

- **Quick Fix**: Spray and wipe the sink and mirror. Done in under 2 minutes.
- **Weekly**: Scrub the toilet, mop the floor, and scrub the shower tiles.

Living Room

- **Quick Fix**: Fluff cushions, fold blankets, and move random junk to its rightful place.
- **Weekly**: Dust, vacuum, and wipe down the coffee table (no one wants sticky rings).

Cleaning Confidence Hacks

- **Music Is Mandatory**: Cleaning without tunes is just boring exercise.
- **Reward Yourself**: For every room cleaned, you earn a Tim Tam (or two).
- **Make It Fun**: Turn cleaning into a game set a timer and see how much you can do in 10 minutes.

Why You've Got This

Cleaning doesn't have to be fancy it just has to work. With your new signature scent, a bottle of vinegar, and a playlist that slaps, you'll be living in a space that smells amazing and looks even better, now grab your mop and channel your inner domestic legend.

Love, Mum

3

Laundry: Isn't That Hard (Promise)

Laundry it's not glamerous, it's not exciting, and yes, it's a bit of a pain. But unless you are ok with wearing the same undies three days in a row (no judgement, just concern), its a non-negotiable part of life. The good news? You don't need a degree in " Washing Machine Science" to pull this off. With a few tips, a bit of effort, and a hell of a playlist you will be cleaning like a pro - or at least like someone who knows not to mix darks with whites.

Your Laundry Essentials (No, a Chair Doesn't Count)

Here's what you actually need to survive laundry day:

- **Laundry Basket**: A.k.a. the "dirty clothes shuttle." Beats carrying a precarious pile of socks, undies, and that hoodie you wore all week.
- **Detergent**: Powder, liquid, or pods. Pick one and don't eat the pods—they're not lollies.
- **Stain Remover**: For those "How on earth did I get tomato sauce THERE?" moments.
- **Drying Rack**: Essential for rainy days or when the housemate hogs the clothesline.
- **Clothes Pegs**: Yes, they're for hanging clothes, not clipping bags of chips closed. (We all do it, though.)
- **Mesh Bags**: Keep your delicates safe from the washing machine's spin cycle of doom.
- **Lint Roller**: Because no one looks cool covered in cat hair—except maybe the cat.

Laundry Basics: Or, How Not to Ruin Everything You Own

Step 1: Sorting (Not Just for the Organised People)

Option 1: Throw it all in and hope for the best. Risky, but hey, you like to live dangerously.
Option 2: Separate whites, darks, and colours. It's less "thrilling," but your whites won't turn pink.
Option 3: Towels and jeans deserve their own wash—they're heavyweights that'll beat up your T-shirts.

Step 2: Washing Machine Settings

Cold Wash: The safest bet. It's gentle on fabrics, colours, and your electricity bill.
Warm Wash: Great for towels, sheets, or the gym clothes you forgot in your bag for a week (gross).
Quick Wash: For when you're short on time or patience but still need clean undies.

Step 3: Drying

Line Drying: The Aussie classic. Fresh air, free sunshine, and fewer wrinkles—your clothes, not your face.
Dryer: The cheat code. Just don't toss in your favourite hoodie unless you're okay with it fitting your dog.

Stain-Rescue 101 (Or, Saving Your Favourite Hoodie)

Oil Stains (The Sneaky Devils)

- Don't panic. Grab flour or baby powder and sprinkle it over the stain ASAP. It'll soak up the oil before it sets.Brush it off, then wash as usual. Crisis averted.
- Dish soap to the rescue cover the stain with dishwashing liquid like you would grease on a pan. Let it sit for 15 minutes scrub gently and rinse before tossing in the wash repeat if needed works like a charm.

Red Wine

- Dab with paper towel (don't rub unless you're aiming for "abstractart"). Pour soda water or white wine on the stain, then wash.
- Salt and boiling water trick block the wine don't rub! Cover with a heap of salt. It'll absorb the red boil water, stretch the stained area over a bowl and slowly pour the hot water from a height being careful as you are using hot water that you don't scold yourself washes normal and look at that it's a miracle.

Foundation on clothes

- Grab yourself some white foamy shaving cream not gel
- Don't rob the foundation with a dry cloth a a squirt of shaving cream to the stain, let it sit for 10 to 15 minutes, then gently scrub with a damp cloth or toothbrush
- Rinse and chuck in the wash
- Bonus tip at a few drops of rubbing alcohol for heavy duty long wearing make up

Deodorant marks

- **Use baby wipe or nylon tight** rub the spot with a pair of nude tights yep weird but works
- Or Swipewipe over it
- Works best on black clothes with those pesky white streak marks love to show up

Ink and not the tattoo type

- Detain with paper towel
- Spray with hairspray or rub in hand sanitiser

- Blocked with clean cloth until ink lifts
- Rinse and wash

Blood don't freak out!

- Never ever use hot water it sets stain
- Make a paste with salt and cold water
- Rub it in gently, let it sit for around 10 minutes rinse and repeat if necessary

Sweat stains gross I know

- Make a paste with bicarb and lemon juice
- Scrub into the armpit area of shirt
- Let it sit for an hour, then wash
- White shirts, Will thank you so will the person see next to you?

Lipstick

- Spray with hairspray
- Let it sit for 10 minutes
- Dub with a dam cloth or sponge
- Repeat if needed before washing

Fabric-Specific Tips (Because Clothes Are Divas)
Towels

Wash them solo in warm water. Skip the fabric softener unless you want them to feel like sandpaper.

Jeans

Turn them inside out before washing. Line dry unless you're ready to rock the "shrunken jeans" look.

Delicates

Toss them in a mesh bag or hand wash. Don't throw them in with your sneakers unless you're feeling chaotic.

Gym Clothes

Wash immediately. Add vinegar to the wash for extra funk-fighting power—because no one likes Eau de Sweat.

Don't Forget the Machines (Yes, They Need TLC Too)

Washing Machine Maintenance

Run an empty cycle with vinegar once a month.
It'll keep things fresh and stop your clothes from smelling like a wet dog. Wipe the rubber seal—because gross things live there, and you don't want to meet them.

Dryer Lint Trap
Empty this after every use. It's not just about efficiency—it's about not accidentally starting a dryer fire.

Laundry Confidence Hacks (AKA Mum's Best Advice)

Hack #1: Set a Timer

- Forgetting your washing is a rookie mistake. A timer stops you from accidentally inventing "mould couture."

Hack #2: Fold It Straight Away

- Mount Clothesmore is preventable. Fold your laundry before it turns into a second couch.

Hack #3: Use the Sun

- Free drying and bacteria-killing magic. Plus, sun-dried sheets are peak Aussie vibes.

Hack #4: Wash Less Often

- Not everything needs to be washed after one wear (jeans and hoodies, I'm looking at you). Unless it smells, save water and effort.

Hack #5: Air It Out

- Got a shirt you wore for 20 minutes? Hang it up to air instead of tossing it in the wash.

Hack #6: Zip and Button Everything

- This stops zips from snagging and buttons from pulling loose.

Hack #7: Outsource When You Must

- Overwhelmed? Some laundromats do a wash-and-fold service. It's like having a magical laundry fairy.

Why You've Got This

Laundry might seem like an endless chore, but it's honestly not that bad once you get the hang of it. Clean clothes make you look good, smell good, and feel like you've got life semi-figured out. So grab your detergent, blast some tunes, and sort that washing—you'll thank yourself later.

Love, Mum

Laundry CHEAT SHEET

WASHING SYMBOLS

machine wash

do not wash

tumble dry

do not tumble dry

WATER TEMPERATURES

cold

warm

hot

quick drying

line drying

SEPARATE LAUNDRY

whites

colors

velcass

delicates

STAIN REMOVAL

blood
cold water

wine
salt, soda water

grease
dish soap

ink
alcohol

Love, Mum

4

Budgeting For People who Hate Maths

Why Budgeting Isn't the Worst Thing Ever

Let's be honest: budgeting isn't exactly the stuff of dreams. No one's waking up thinking, "I can't wait to compare my spending on groceries versus Uber Eats today!" But here's the kicker—it's actually pretty empowering. Think of it like giving your money a map and a purpose, so it doesn't just vanish into thin air (or the Macca's drive-thru). With a few tips and some mum-approved wisdom, you'll be budgeting like a pro in no time.

Know Where Your Money's Going (Spoiler: Probably Starbucks coffee)

Before you can start budgeting, you've got to figure out where your cash is sneaking off to. Spoiler: it's probably Starbucks coffee…. and the toasted cream cheese bagel.

Track Your Spending

- Use a free tool from your bank. NAB, CommBank, and most Aussie banks offer budgeting features and charts that break down your spending into categories—groceries, entertainment, "oh my god, why did I spend $80 on candles? "Or, go old-school with a notebook. Write down *everything* you spend for a week—even the servo sausage roll. Yes, that too.
- By the end of the week, you'll see where your money is going and which habits need tweaking (no judgment, just reality).
- There is also lots of apps and government websites that help with this as well.

Free apps and government budgeting apps

- **Moneysmart** budget planner by ASIC government platform website and mobile friendly. **What it does….** is a straightforward, no-frills budgeting tool that helps you plan where your money goes. Enter your income, expenses, and savings goals then print, download or email your results. **Why it's good….** It has no ads no selling just solid Aussie advice but by ASIC link **moneysmart.gov.au**
- **WiseList** platform iOS and android W**hat it does……** combines grocery tracking, budgeting, bill, reminders, and shopping list management all in one. Helps you keep track of spending, especially at the supermarket. **Why is it good…..** Aussie developed integrate Coles and woollies prices to help

you find a cheaper options free with optional premium up-grades link **wiselist.app**
- **We money** platform iOS and android **What it does**.... synced to your bank accounts and helps track spending, set budget, view credit scores, and join us supportive financial community. **Why it's good**.... easy to use, Australian based, visually appealing, includes bill tracking, free with optional premium features.
- **Frollo** platform iOS and android **What it does**.... connects all your financial accounts using open baking tech, give you real time insight, spending breakdowns, and goal tracking. **Why it's good**... secure, australian, and built on responsible finance principles. Great for people serious about budgeting and goal setting link. **frollo.com.au**

Bonus Tip .... Spot the Trends in your spending

- Are you buying more iced coffees than actual groceries? Spending more on subscriptions than petrol? This step isn't about guilt—it's about awareness. Knowledge is power, kids.

The 50-30-20 Rule (AKA Budgeting for People Who Hate Math)

This is budgeting made simple:

- **50% Needs**: Rent, groceries, bills, petrol—stuff you can't live without.
- **30% Wants**: Netflix, eating out, those funky socks you absolutely didn't need but bought anyway.
- **20% Savings**: This is for future-you, who will absolutely love you for it one day.

Mum Tip:

Set up three bank accounts—one for each category—and transfer the money as soon as you get paid.
It's like meal prepping but for your finances.
Coles sale swap over happens evey wednesday

Save Without Suffering

Saving doesn't mean you have to live off baked beans and toast (although shoutout to baked beans—underrated legends).
Here's how to save without hating your life:

The Round-Up Hack

- Alot of Aussie banks let you round up purchases to the nearest dollar and throw the spare change into savings. It's sneaky savings at its finest. So what is the round up hack in essence it is an account that helps you save money without thinking about it, when you buy something using your bank card, the bank round up the amount to the nearest dollar and put the extra money into your savings.
- **Example:** you buy coffee for **$3.50** the Bank round up to **$4** that extra **$.50** go straight into your savings account.
- **Why is this great?** Well it's automatic, you don't need to do anything, it adds up fast. Even small purchases build up a saving stash, you don't notice it's missing. It's like digital spare change..

What's a Round-Up Account?

A round-up account helps you save money without thinking about it.

Example:

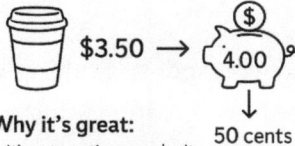

$3.50 → 4.00

50 cents

Why it's great:
- It's automatic – you don't need to do anything
- It adds up fast – even small purchases build a savings stash
- You don't notice it missing – it's like digital spare change

Please note you do need to check with your bank if they actually offer this feature not all banks offer it although a lot do.

The $5 Rule

- Every time you get a $5 note, stash it in a jar. Watch it grow. Use it for emergencies, or for something fun—like a surprise Kmart spree.
- **How it works** buy a coffee, get five dollars change, save the five dollar note, grab lunch, break a $20 note save the five dollar note you keep doing this every time you get a fiver until you've got a nice little stash of emergency money, holiday cash, or guilt free splurge fund.
- **Why it works** it's so small, you don't really notice that it's gone, but it adds up fast. Save just 2 x $5 notes a week and you've got $520 a year, it's physical, it's visual watching it grow is motivation.

The One-Week Rule

- Thinking of buying something you don't *really* need? Wait a week. If you still want it, go for it. If not, congrats—you just saved yourself $50.
- **How it works** Say you spot something you want new shoes, a gadget, random online cart items, instead of buying it on the spot write it down or take a screenshot. Set a reminder for seven days later, if you still want it just as much and can afford it go for it, if you've moved on or forgotten about it you just save money.
- **So why does this work** Stops impulse buying, give your brain time to decide if it's a need or just a want (guess what most of the time its just a want). It help you spend with intention, emotion and makes you more mindful with your money. What does that do that equals more left for things you truly value.

How to Spend Smarter (So You Can Save Harder)

Grocery Shopping Like a Pro

- **Make a List**: And actually stick to it. Those "middle aisles" are designed to trick you into buying snacks you don't need (looking at you, Tim Tams).
- **hop the Specials**: Download the Woolies or Coles app and stock up on half-price goodies. There's no shame in bulk-buying loo paper go to Aldi and the reject shop they often have amazing prices on necessities —it's just smart.
- **Don't Shop Hungry**: Unless you want to end up with three tubs of ice cream and no bread.

Don't Fear Secondhand

- Facebook Marketplace, Gumtree, and op shops are full of treasures. You could furnish your entire house for less than the cost of a new couch.

Kill the Subscriptions

- Do you really need Netflix, Disney+, Stan, *and* Spotify? Pick one. Or find a mate willing to "lend" you their login. Sharing is caring, cash in on student subscriptionsloads of places and companies offer students really great discounts.

The Great Takeaway Compromise

- Limit yourself to one takeaway night a week, but make it count—get the extra chips or spring for dessert.

Debt: The Fun Sponge

Debt is like glitter—it's hard to get rid of, and it shows up everywhere. Let's tackle it:

- **Smallest First**: Knock out the smallest debt first. It's satisfying, and the "snowball method" works.
- **Credit Card Hack**: Pay it off in full every month. If you can't, put the card in a drawer and pretend it doesn't exist. Or better still, don't get one!
- **Buy Now, Pay Later?**: No. Just no. It's a trap. If you can't afford it now, save up for it instead.
- **Phone bills and internet:** If you can opt for pre paid you top up once a month it's a set amount and you don't find yourself with high a bill, companies like "boost", "belong" and many others offer great rates with more than, enough data makes life a

lot easier, and no need to enter into long term contracts that stay on your credit file.

Emergency Fund: Your Safety Net

Think of this as your "Oh Crap" fund—money for when life happens. Car repairs, surprise bills, last-minute festival tickets, you get the idea.
Start with $1,000 if possible and build from there no shame in starting with $50 it all matters.

How to Build It Fast

- **Sell Stuff**: That barely-used guitar or old PlayStation could be someone else's treasure—and your ticket to an emergency fund.
- **Side Hustle**: Deliver pizzas, babysit, freelance, catalogue drops or dog-walk your way to a safety net.
- **Surveys:** If your going to sit there on your phone why dont you sign up, do surveys and get paid for it the internet is full of le-gitament companies offering cash rewards.

Budgeting Confidence Hacks

- **Automate Everything**: Bills, savings, rent—set it and forget it. You can't spend money that's already gone.
- **Reward Yourself**: Stuck to your budget for a whole month? Treat yourself. Balance is key.
- **Focus on Progress, Not Perfection**: Even saving $10 a week is better than nothing. Small wins add up.

Why You've Got This

Budgeting might not sound exciting, but it's the key to living your best life. It's not about saying no to everything fun—it's about saying yes to the stuff that really matters.
Stick with it, and you'll have money for what you need,
what you want, and a little extra for the things you never saw coming.

Love, Mum

BUDGETING CHEAT SHEET

Needs vs. Wants

Things you need to survive (e g. food, rent, chilli sauce)

Wants Things that are nice but not essential.

Don't forget to save for something special, like a cheeky avo toast or a night out with your mates!

The 50/30/20 Rule

50% Needs

30% Savings

20% Savings

Monthly Budget Checklist

Keep a tab on your spending, love.

Savings Tips

Make it a habit and watch those dollars grow!

Emergency Fund

Set up a buffer for unexpected expenses

Love, Mum

5

Bills Made Easy

Why Bills Don't Have to Be Scary

Ah, bills the uninvited guests in your letterbox (or inbox) that seem to pop up just when you thought you had your money sorted. The good news? They're not out to get you they're just part of being a grown-up. The better news? With a bit of planning, paying them doesn't have to feel like a financial punch to the face. Let's break it down so you can spend less time stressing and more time living.

The Big Three Bills (And How to Tame Them)

1. Rent/ Mortgage

- Rent is probably your biggest expense, and the one you *cannot* forget (unless you enjoy camping).
- **(Mum Tip:** Set up a direct debit for your rent so it comes out automatically ideally as soon as you get paid. (No one wants an awkward chat with their landlord.)
- If you're renting with housemates, make one person "rent captain" to collect everyone's share. Bonus: you get to wear a metaphorical captain's hat.

2. Utilities (Electricity, Water, Gas)

- These bills can sneak up on you like a huntsman in the shower, so don't ignore them.
- **Mum Tip:** Sign up for e-billing so you don't lose them under a pile of junk mail.
- Compare providers every year websites like Energy Made Easy can help you find cheaper deals faster than you can say, "Do I really need aircon on 24/7?"

3. Internet and Phone

- You're going to need these unless you plan to live like it's 1995.
- **Mum Tip:** Bundle your internet and phone together if it saves you money. Also, watch out for sneaky extra fees no one needs a $400 phone bill, because they forgot to turn off mobile data?.

How to Budget for Bills Without Losing Your Mind

1. Know Your Due Dates

- Get all your bill due dates into a calendar or app (Google Calendar works a treat). Add reminders so you're not hit with late fees.
- **Mum Procrastination Hack:** Set reminders for a few days *before* the due date, so you don't leave it to the last minute like that Year 12 English assignment.

2. Estimate and Split

- Add up your monthly bills, divide by four, and stash that amount away weekly. It's like meal-prepping, but for your wallet.
- **Mum Math Moment:** If your bills total $400 a month, set aside $100 a week. Bam money's ready when the bills hit.

3. Use Separate Accounts

- Open a "bills-only" bank account. Transfer your weekly bill money there so it doesn't accidentally turn into takeaway sushi money.

Save on Bills (Because Every Dollar Counts)

Electricity and Gas

- Turn off lights when you leave the room you're not running a nightclub.
- Switch to energy-efficient globes. They last forever and don't make your wallet cry.

- Use appliances off-peak if your plan allows it (think late-night laundry parties).
- If the bill comes in high make sure to check meter usage this can be done by looking at your meter or checking the webpage of your elctricity company.

Water

- Shorten your showers. I know it's your personal karaoke stage, but the planet and your water bill will thank you.
- Is there leaks.? A dripping tap isn't just annoying it's money literally going down the drain.

Internet and Phone

- Shop around for deals. Telcos are like that clingy ex they'll offer you better rates if you even *think* about switching.
- Limit data usage. Do you really need to watch videos in HD?
- As mentioned in the previous section think about prepaid it makes life much easier and sets a manageable amount for you, if you do need to top up extra data you are in control of how much to spend not the other way around.

When a Bill Is Late (Don't Panic!) It happens. Here's what to do:

1. **Call Them**: Companies would rather work with you than chase you, so don't be afraid to pick up the phone.
2. **Ask for a Payment Plan**: Many companies will let you pay in smaller chunks if you're struggling.
3. **Set a New System**: If this keeps happening, go back to Step 2: Budget for Bills and fix your setup.

Mum's Pro Tips to Stay Ahead

The Power of Auto-Pay

- Set up direct debits for bills that are the same every month (like Netflix). For variable bills, set a reminder so you don't forget.

Keep a Buffer Fund

- Stash $200-$500 in a "bill buffer" account. This is for surprise price hikes or when you accidentally leave the heater on all night.

Pay Weekly or Fortnightly

- Some companies let you pay smaller amounts regularly instead of one big lump sum. Less stress, same result.

Don't Be Afraid to Haggle

- Call your provider once a year and ask if they can give you a better deal. Mention you're "thinking of switching," and watch the discounts roll in.

What About Unexpected Bills?

Life happens. The car breaks down, the dog swallows a sock, or your phone takes a swim in the toilet. Here's how to handle it:

- **Emergency Fund**: That stash you've been building? Now's the time to use it.
- **Payment Plans**: Most companies are happy to work something out. Call them and explain the situation.
- **Mum Advice**: Take a deep breath. You'll get through it.

Why You've Got This

Bills might seem boring, but they're actually pretty manageable once you've got a system, with a little planning, some clever hacks, and maybe a few cheeky discounts,you'll be on top of your finances in no time. Remember: you're the boss of your money, not the other way around.

Love, Mum

Bills Made Easy –
– Cheat Sheet

1. Know What's Coming

- Rent/Mortgage
- Electricity
- Gas
- Water
- Internet/Phone
- Streaming services
- Insurance (car, home, health)
- Car rego
- Credit cards/Loans

2. Work Out the Due Dates

Use a calendar or bill tracking app
Highlight monthly vs quarterly vs yearly bills

3. Automate Payments

- Set up direct debits or BPAY
- One less thing to remember!

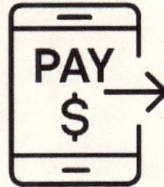

PAY
$

4. Split the Cost

- Set up weekly/fortnightly payments
- Cover a bit of each bill, each pay

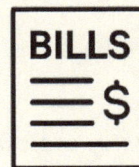

BILLS
$

6

Grocery Hacks

Grocery Shopping Doesn't Have to Be a Nightmare

Grocery shopping is like adulting on hard mode. You start with big plans ("I'll cook every night and save heaps!") but end up buying instant noodles, a $12 block of cheese, and no actual meals. If you're living out of home for the first time, the struggle is real, but don't worry—Mum's got your back. With some clever tips, a little planning, and a sense of humour, you'll crush your next shop without crushing your budget.

Step 1: The Grocery Game Plan

Make a List (And Stick to It, I Mean It)

- Before you go, write down exactly what you need. Think of it as your battle plan for the wild jungle of the supermarket.
- Mum Tip: Put snacks on the list, because let's be real, you'll buy them anyway. Might as well make them intentional.

Shop Your Pantry First

- Check your cupboards before you head out. There's nothing worse than buying rice or pasta only to discover you've already got enough to feed a small army.

Don't Shop Hungry

- Hungry you is an impulsive spender. Suddenly, everything looks delicious, you walk out with six tubs of ice cream and no bread. Eat before you shop.

Step 2: Navigating the Supermarket Like a Pro

Beware the Middle Aisles

- The middle aisles are where dreams and budgets go to die. Stick to the edges of the store—that's where the fresh stuff like fruit, veg, and bread lives.

Compare Prices Like a Boss

- Look at the price per 100g or per litre on the shelf tags. It's the secret weapon for spotting sneaky rip-offs.

Aldi = Your New Best Friend

- Aldi is the holy grail of cheap groceries. Their pantry staples, snacks, and random weekly "Special Buys" (camping gear? a bread maker?) are unbeatable.

Don't Forget The Reject Shop, Costco and Amazon

- For essentials like laundry powder, dish soap, and even snacks, The Reject Shop is a hidden gem. You'll save heaps, and sometimes you'll even find name-brand items for half the price.

Step 3: Saving Like a Legend

Embrace Home Brands

- Supermarket home brands are just as good as the fancy stuff. Trust me, your pasta sauce doesn't care what label the tin had.

Shop the Specials

- Check the catalogues or apps before you go. If chicken thighs are half-price, guess what's for dinner this week?

BYO Bags (and Trolley Token)

- Not only will you save on those sneaky bag fees, but you'll also look like you've got your life together. And don't forget a coin or token for the trolley—no one wants to be that person awkwardly trying to free one.

Bulk-Buy Wisely

- Pantry staples like rice, flour, and tinned tomatoes are great to buy in bulk. But unless you're running a café, skip the 5kg tub of mayonnaise.

Step 4: Meal Planning Without Losing Your Soul

Plan Around What's Cheap

- If mince is on sale, it's spaghetti, tacos, and shepherd's pie week. Think versatile ingredients that can be used for multiple meals. Some examples are at the end of this chapter.

Cook Once, Eat Twice

- Double your recipes and freeze the extras. Future-you will be eternally grateful when dinner is as simple as defrosting dinner already cooked not to mention its handy if you have had a bit of a budget blow out and you need dinner.

Use Your Leftovers

- Roast a chicken, and use the leftovers for sandwiches, wraps, or a quick stir-fry. Mum Tip: Toss the carcass into a pot with some veggies for a homemade soup that'll make you feel like a pro.

Mum's Grocery Hacks

Hack #1: Shop Alone

- Supermarkets are not social venues. Friends will pressure you into buying fancy cheese and unnecessary snacks. Go solo for maximum focus.

Hack #2: Be Strategic

- Hit the freezer section last so your ice cream doesn't turn into soup before you get home.

Hack #3: The "Mum Scan"

- Before checkout, do a final trolley scan. If you're questioning the $10 bag of kale chips, put it back.

Hack #4: Hunt the Clearance Stickers

- Bread, meat, and veggies often get discounted at the end of the day. It's like a treasure hunt, but tastier, if you don't need it right now put it straight into the freezer and use another time.

What About Online Shopping?

Online = Lazy Genius

- If you hate crowds, online shopping is your best mate.
- **Sort by Specials**: Most sites let you filter for discounts. Do this first.
- **Click and Collect**: Saves you the delivery fee and the hassle of navigating the aisles.

- **Don't Get Sucked In**: No, you don't need the $30 "luxury hamper" to get $20 off your shop they suggest at checkout.

Why You've Got This

Grocery shopping might seem like an overwhelming chore, but it's also an opportunity to flex your independence and save some cash. With a bit of planning, some savvy hacks, and a cheeky Aldi Special Buy or two, you'll have a full fridge, a stocked pantry, and money left for the important stuff (like actual food or the occasional splurge).

You've got this, legend.

Love, Mum

Multi-Meal
INGREDIENT LIST

🍗 PROTEINS

- **Chicken thighs or breasts**
- List in s' trir-fries, tacos, wraps, soups, salads & baken

- **Canned chickpeas or lentils**
- Curries, salads, wraps, soups, veggie burgers

- Stir-fries, tocos pasta, wraps soups, salads

- Curries, salads wraps, soups veggie burgers

🥕 VEGETABLES

- **Frozen mixed veg or stir-fry pack**
- **Baby spinach**
- **Capsicum (bell pepper)**

- Fried rice, curry burrito bowls
- Rice pudding
- Stir-fry, rurry

🧀 GRAINS & BASES

- **Rice** (white or brown)
- **Pasta**
- **Tortillas or wraps**

- Pasta sauce, curry
- Chilli, soup
- Shakshuka

🧄 FRIDGE/PANTRY STAPLES

- **Tinned tomatoes**
- **Cheese** (like tasty or mozzarella
- **Garlic & onion**
- **Greek yoghurt** the base of most tasty meals

- Toasties, pasta wraps, baked potatoes, nachos

7

Fix It: Why Your Allowed to Panic

But only for a second

Life in Australia isn't all sunshine and barbies sometimes the tap leaks, the power goes out, or your phone takes a dive into the backyard pool. These moments aren't fun, but they're fixable. With a bit of calm, some basic tools, and a splash of Aussie ingenuity, you'll be able to tackle most of life's little curveballs without needing to call Mum (unless you really want to, in which case, go ahead 'll answer).

Fix It Basics: The Golden Rules

Stay Calm

- Freaking out never fixed a burst hose or a burnt dinner. Take a breath and channel your inner Steve Irwin calm, resourceful, and ready for action.

Assess the Damage

- Is this a quick DIY fix, or do you need professional help? Hint: If it involves live wires, call someone who knows what they're doing.

Google and YouTube Are Gold

- There's a tutorial for *everything*. Need to unblock a sink or patch a hole in the wall? The internet's got your back.

Call in the Cavalry

- If it's beyond you, don't stress. Whether it's a tradie, a house-mate, or a mate who owes you a favour, help is just a call away.

Common Household Disasters

Leaky Tap

- **What to Do**:

1. Tighten the tap (righty-tighty, lefty-loosey).
2. If it's still dripping, turn off the water at the mains (usually near the front of the house).
3. Call a plumber if it's more than a dribble.

- **Mum Tip**: Put a bucket under the drip to save water—it's liquid gold, especially in summer. Use it to water your plants or clean the balcony.

Power Outage

- **What to Do**:

1. Grab a torch always keep one handy because phones die fast.
2. Check if it's just your house (look out the window are the neighbours' lights on?).
3. Check your fuse box and flip any tripped switches. If that doesn't work, call your energy provider.

- **Mum Wisdom**: Keep the fridge and freezer closed. Food stays colder longer when you're not peeking.

Clogged Toilet

- **What to Do**:

1. Use a plunger (buy one, trust me).
2. If it's stubborn, pour hot water and dish soap into the bowl. Wait a few minutes, then try plunging again.
3. If it's still clogged, call a plumber before things get… messy.

- **Mum Tip**: Never flush wipes, cotton buds, or the receipt for the shoes you're returning.

Outdoor Fix-Its: The Extra Edition

Broken Fly Screen

- **What to Do:**

1. Grab some flyscreen mesh and a staple gun (Bunnings, your new best mate).
2. Cut the mesh to size, staple it into place, and feel like a DIY god.

- **Mum Wisdom:** A good fly screen is the only thing standing between you and a house full of mozzies.

Gutter Overflowing

- **What to Do:**

1. Put on gloves and scoop out the leaves.
2. Hose down the gutter to clear any leftover gunk.

- **Mum Tip:** Check after storms clogged gutters can cause leaks faster than you can say "summer rain."

Dead Lawn

- **What to Do:**

1. Water it deeply once or twice a week (not every day it's Australia, not England).
2. Sprinkle lawn seed and let nature do its thing.

- **Mum Wisdom:** Accept that some Aussie lawns will always look a bit "crispy" in summer.

Car Troubles: What Now? Remember Safety always FIRST

Flat Tyre

- **What to Do:**

1. Pull over somewhere safe and turn on your hazards, try to be as far over as possible to increase the space between you and the cars driving past.
2. Grab your spare tyre and jack from the boot.
3. Follow a YouTube tutorial if you're stuck or call the NRMA. There is no shame in feeling more comfortable to call roadside assistance… (Truthfully I would.).

- **Mum Tip:** Practice changing a tyre on a sunny day, not when you're stuck on the Hume Highway in the rain.

Dead Battery

- **What to Do:**

1. Grab jumper leads and find someone to help it's always a good idea to carry a set of jumper leads in your car these can be purchased from super cheap auto or any car supply pace they don't need to be the most expensive just something to get the job done.
2. Connect the cables (positive to positive (red is dead "you"),then negative to negative (black to booster battery other car).
3. Start the other car first, then yours once your car is running disconnect the negative cables from your battery first then from the other car.
4. Disconnect the positive cable (red) from the working car first ten disconnect the positive cable from your car.

5. Let your car run ideally for about 30 min before driving DO NOT TURN THE CAR OFF STRAIGHT AWAY ONCE JUMP STARTED!

• **Mum Wisdom**: Turn off the headlights when you park. Classic rookie mistake.

Tech Fixes: The Mum Cheat Sheet

Phone in Water

• **What to Do**:

1. Turn it off immediately.
2. Dry it thoroughly, then bury it in rice or silica gel packets if you have them overnight.

• **Mum Wisdom**: Maybe don't take your phone into the bathroom. Just a thought.

Extra Fix-It Tips: The Bonus Round

Scratched Floorboards

• **What to Do**:

1. Rub a walnut (yes, the nut) over the scratch. The natural oils help fill it in.
2. If you don't have walnuts lying around (fair), use a crayon in a similar colour, then buff it with a cloth.

3. Still visible? Touch it up with a furniture marker (Bunnings sells them cheap).

- **Mum Wisdom**: Rugs are the ultimate scratch cover-up. Also, pets and heels are floorboards' mortal enemies plan accordingly.

Wobbly Chair or Table

- **What to Do**:

1. Check for loose screws and tighten them.
2. If it's still wobbly, stick a folded piece of cardboard or a coaster under the short leg.

- **Mum Tip**: Blu Tack works in a pinch, but don't use half the pack unless you want it stuck forever.

Stubborn Stickers on Glass

- **What to Do**:

1. Soak the sticker with white vinegar or eucalyptus oil. Let it sit for a minute.
2. Scrape it off with an old gift card or your nails if you're brave.

- **Mum Wisdom**: Don't use a knife unless you want to scratch the glass *and* your finger.

Holes in the Wall

- **What to Do**:

1. Fill small holes with toothpaste (white, not minty fresh).

2. Let it dry, then lightly sand it smooth.
3. For bigger holes, grab some spackle and follow a quick YouTube tutorial.

- **Mum Tip**: Toothpaste is a temporary fix. If you're renting, invest in proper filler before the landlord's inspection.

Stained Coffee Table

- **What to Do**:

1. Mix a paste of bicarb soda and water.
2. Rub it into the stain gently, then wipe clean with a damp cloth.
3. For stubborn marks, a little bit of toothpaste can do wonders.

- **Mum Wisdom**: Coasters aren't just for decoration, kids.

Leaky Tap

- Already in here, but don't forget to tighten all connections under the sink sometimes it's just a loose nut (not you, the plumbing).

Squeaky Door Hinges

- **What to Do**:

1. Spray some WD-40 or rub a bit of olive oil on the hinge.
2. Open and close the door a few times to work it in.

- **Mum Wisdom**: If the squeak's back in a week, it's just the door saying hi.

Stubborn Lightbulb

• **What to Do**:

1. Turn off the power at the switchboard (seriously, safety first).
2. Use a rubber glove for extra grip, and twist gently.

• **Mum Wisdom**: Always keep spare lightbulbs on hand. Your future self will thank you.

Scratched Glass

• **What to Do**:

1. Use a dab of toothpaste (not gel) on the scratch.
2. Rub it in circles with a soft cloth, then wipe clean.
3. Works best on small scratches don't expect miracles for your windscreen.

• **Mum Wisdom**: Toothpaste fixes everything, but don't start brushing your walls, okay?

Mum's Ultimate Fix-It Kit

Every household should have these essentials:

• **Duct Tape**: Fixes everything from cracked hoses to broken broom handles.
• **WD-40**: Stops squeaks and loosens stuck bolts.
• **Torch and Batteries**: For blackouts and late-night hunts for the remote under the couch. Remember to have AA and AAA on hand some times you may need C size battery for your torch always have spare on hand.

- **Bicarb Soda and Vinegar**: Nature's problem solvers for cleaning drains, scrubbing tiles, and de-funking gym gear.
- **Walnuts**: For scratched wood. Also a healthy snack look at you, multitasking.
- **Eucalyptus Oil**: Removes sticky residue and smells like you've been to the spa.
- **Toothpaste**: The MVP of household hacks. Fixes walls, glass, and even your reputation (as long as you remember to use it on your teeth too).
- **Rubber Gloves**: For grip, cleaning, and making you look like you know what you're doing.
- **Superglue**: Fixes everything from broken mugs to wobbly fridge magnets.
- **Basic Toolkit**: Screwdrivers, a hammer, nails, and a measuring tape no, your phone app doesn't count.

Why You've Got This

Life's little disasters are just that little. Whether it's a scratch, a squeak, or a full-blown plumbing crisis, you've got
the tools, the skills, and the can-do attitude to handle it.
Remember: nothing's truly broken until you give up on it,
and even then, there's probably a way to hide it until inspection day.
Now go out there and fix it you got this.

Love, Mum

8

Health Tips: Mum Can't Be Your Doctor Forever

When you're young, it's easy to think you're invincible. Late nights, dodgy kebabs, and ignoring your annual check-up seem like no big deal—until they are. Staying healthy isn't about giving up fun; it's about making sure you can keep having it. With a few simple habits, you can look after your body, your mind, and your spirit (and avoid those awkward doctor lectures Mum used to save you from).

The Basics (A Mum's Eye View)

Drink Water

- Your body needs water. Coffee, energy drinks, and soft drinks don't count. Aim for at least 2 liters a day—more if it's hot or you've been running around like a headless chook.
- **Mum Tip**: Keep a reusable bottle with you fun fact warm/ hot water is actually better for your body than cold. Bonus: it makes you look like you've got your life together.

Get Some Sleep

- **7-9 hours a night;** No excuses. Netflix will still be there tomorrow, spoiler alert not getting enough sleep is more than just being a bit cranky.
- **Your brain gets foggy;** Think slow Wi-Fi and 30 open tabs concentrating gets harder, and your memory gone. You'll forget your keys your passwords and what you walked into the room for.
- **Your immune system weakens;** catching every cold flu and mystery bug going round that's your sleep deprived body waving the white flag
- **You crave junk;** your body wants energy, so it tricks you into eating chips, sugar, and all the carbs but does it help note just makes you hungry and bloated.
- **Your skin cops it;** hello dark circles, dull skin, and surprise pimples your body repairs itself during sleep skip it and you start looking like a zombie who lost a fight
- **Stress hits harder;** lack of sleep jacks up your cortisol. That's your stress hormone small problems feel huge big problems feel like a apocalypse.
- **You get moody and no it's not just a bad day;** Lack of sleep messes with your emotions one second you're fine. The next

you're crying over drop biscuit your tolerance for people non-existent.

- **You're slower physically and mentally;** reaction times drop mistakes go up your trip over nothing send emails to the wrong person and forget where you parked
- **You risk long-term health issues;** consistent sleep deprivation has been linked to heart problems, weight gain, diabetes, and even depression. It's no joke.

When to Worry (and When to Chill)

Fevers and Temperatures

What even is a fever?

- A fever is when your body temp hits 38° or higher. It's your body's way of saying oh something is not right I'm fighting it off. Your body normally sits around 36.5° to 37.5° when something is not right like a virus, bacterial infection, or inflammation your internal thermostat turns up the heat to help fight it off. Think of like putting your immune system into turbo mode heat slows down the growth of the virus and bacteria. It helps your immune system cells move faster and work better. It cooks out invaders so your body can win the fight. It's uncomfortable but it's not always a bad thing. It means your body is working.

When to Chill:

- A slight fever (37.5–38.5°C) is usually your body fighting something off. Rest, drink water, and let it do its thing.
- Moderate fever 39° to 39.9 is classified a moderate fever however it's always good to keep an eye on any temperature that goes to 39° and over and won't come down.

When to Worry:

- If it's 39°C or higher.
- If it lasts more than 2 days.
- It doesn't go down with paracetamol or ibuprofen. You're taking something, waited the recommended time, and the temperature still climbing that's your cue.
- You've got other health issues if you have a weak immune system, asthma, diabetes, or a history of health complications. Don't wait it out. Call the doctor early.
- High fevers of 40° to 41°. This is when things start getting serious you'll probably feel wiped out achy or confused. **Seek help.**
- If it comes with other symptoms like a stiff neck, rash, or difficulty breathing.
- Hyperpyrexia over 41° **medical emergency your body can't function well at this time go to the hospital immediately**
- **Mum Tip**: A digital thermometer is your best mate. Stick one in your first aid kit.

Who to contact Australia

- **Health direct Australia;** 1800 022 222
- **000;** if someone is unresponsive can't breathe properly or is deteriorating fast, call this number immediately.
- **Local GP;** book an urgent appointment or a walk-in most places unless rural have a medical Centre somewhere.
- **Telehealth consultations;** such as Instascript www.instascripts.com.au

Pain That Doesn't Go Away

- **Track it down;** Where is it? What kind of pain is it sharp? Dull, burning, throbbing.
- **When does it show up?** All the time? When you sit? Stand? Walk?
- **What makes it worse? what helps to ease it off?** this Info helps the Dr actually help you instead of guessing.
- **A headache after a long day**? Normal. A headache that feels like a marching band is in your skull and sticks around for days? Not normal—get it checked out.
- **Has the pain lasted longer than 3 to 5 days?** if yes and it's not easing up, time to book a doctors appointment
- **Ask yourself** is it stopping you from sleeping? Is it making it hard to work or do normal things? Are you getting headaches fatigue or Moodswings from it? Does it keep coming back in the same spot if yes to any of these get checked.
- **Rule out the serious persistent pain** might be muscular or joint related example information, injury, posture issues.
- **Nerve pain** burning, electric zap, kind of pain
- **Referred pain** from an organ example gallbladder, heart, kidneys

- **Chronic pain** conditions like endometriosis, arthritis, or fibromyalgia
- **Mental health** related stress and anxiety can manifest as real physical pain.

Cuts and Scrapes

When to Chill:

- Most minor cuts can be cleaned, bandaged, and forgotten.
- **Wash your hands first** before you touch anything especially the wound give your hands a scrub we're cleaning the cup not adding extra gems to it.
- **Stop the bleeding** don't panic apply gentle, firm pressure with a clean cloth or paper towel and elevate the area if it's bleeding a lot, it should stop within a few minutes if it doesn't get it looked at.
- **Clean the wound** properly rinse it gently under clean running water. Use a mild soap around the wound.
- **Use an antiseptic** wipe or solution like Betadine Savlon or the Dettol the diluted kind this step is important, don't skip it just because it stings a bit. You'll thank yourself later when it doesn't get infected.
- **Cover it** small scrapes leave it to the air, if you're staying clean **deeper cut** or anything near your clothes, dirt cover with a sterile bandage or plaster. Change the dressing daily or as soon as it gets wet.
- **Keep an eye on it** signs of infection to watch out for a redness that spreads, swelling, pus, gross but important to note, throbbing pain, warm skin around the area, fever in more serious cases if anything feels off get it checked.

When to Worry:

- If it's deep, won't stop bleeding after 10 minutes, or looks infected (red, swollen, or oozing).
- If the cut was caused by rusty Nail, dirty object, or animal bite and you haven't had a tetanus shot in the last 5 to 10 years get to the doctor better a jab in the arm than an emergency later.
- There's something stuck in it that you can't get out, this is the time to go to the doctor or the emergency ward.
- The wound starts smelling funny, oozing weird stuff or hurting worse instead of better.
- You feel unwell in general.

Vomiting and Diarrhoea

When to Chill and What to do:

- A one-off bout might just be something you ate.
- If you're vomiting or running to the loo every 10 minutes, don't go anywhere not school, not to work, not to woollies you need rest and nobody else needs your germs.
- Focus on hydration first the biggest danger with vomiting and diarrhoea is dehydration. You lose fluids fast when things are coming out both ends take small sips of water frequently try electrolyte drinks like hydro light Gastro light or even icy poles. If that's all you can keep down avoid juice, fizzy drinks, caffeine, or milk at first they can make things worse.
- Don't force food too soon. Your gut needs a minute. When you're ready to eat again keep a gentle safe foods dry toast, plain crackers, boiled rice, bananas, steamed or mashed potato, and clear soup or broth like a bone broth.
- Let it run its course. Literally most cases are viral Gastro and clear up in 24 to 72 hours. Avoid medications like Imodium un-

less the doctor recommends it it can trap the virus in your system. Your body is trying to get rid of something. Let it.

- Keep things very clean it's highly contagious, so treat your bathroom like a crime scene wash hands properly use disinfectant wipes, or sprays on toilet services, taps, and door handles separate towels, cups, and cutlery, wash soiled clothes or sheets on a hot cycle if possible, if not hang them outside in the fresh air sun is wonderful at getting rid of germs and bacteria.

When to Worry:

- Can't keep fluids down for more than 8 to 12 hours.
- Vomiting last more than two days or diarrhoea more than 3 to 4 days.
- Blood in vomit or poo.
- Signs of dehydration dry mouth, sunken eyes, no wee for 8+ hours.
- Fever over 39°, or lasting longer than two days.
- If you're feeling really unwell and dizzy, weak, confused, or just not right.
- For babies or toddlers, call your doctor sooner they dehydrate quickly and need watching.

What to Do in Basic Emergencies

It is always a good idea to invest in the ST JOHNS FIRST AID BOOK.

Burns

- Run the burn under cool (not cold) water for at least 20 minutes. Don't use ice—it can make it worse.
- Cover with a clean, non-stick dressing.
- See a doctor if it blisters or covers a large area.

Choking

- If they can cough, encourage them to keep coughing—it's the body's way of clearing the blockage.
- If they can't cough or breathe, call **000** immediately and perform the Heimlich manoeuvre (look up a quick video now—knowledge is power). DO NOT PAT THEIR BACK IN CAN LODGE IT FURTHER DOWN.

Sprains and Strains

- RICE: Rest, Ice, Compression, Elevation.
- If it still hurts after a couple of days or swells like a balloon, get it checked out.

Nosebleeds

- Sit upright (don't tilt your head back—trust me, it's gross).
- Pinch your nose just below the bridge for 10 minutes.
- If it doesn't stop after 20 minutes, seek medical help.

Eat Like a Grown-Up (Most of the Time)

- You don't have to live on kale and quinoa, but veggies, protein, and carbs belong on your plate. The occasional Tim Tam is fine—just don't make it the whole meal.
- **Mum Wisdom**: Learn to cook a few simple, healthy meals. Your future self (and your bank account) will thank you.

Moving Your Body (No, Walking to the Fridge Doesn't Count)

Find What You Enjoy

- Hate the gym? Try dancing, hiking, swimming, or team sports. Exercise isn't a punishment—it's about finding something you actually like.
- **Mum Tip**: Take a walk after dinner. It's good for digestion and gives you time to clear your head.

Make It a Habit

- You don't need to train like an Olympian. Aim for 30 minutes of movement most days, whether it's yoga in your room or kicking a footy around with mates.

Moving Your Body (Safely and Smartly)

Walking, Jogging, or Hiking (PLEASE REFER TO HIKING SAFELY SECTION OF THIS BOOK)

- **Stay aware of your surroundings.**
- **Stick to well-lit areas** at night avoid shortcuts through bus trails, alleyway, or random open field especially at dusk or dark choose foot pals, tracks you know, or bushy Park loops where others are around.
- **Keep one ear free** if you're listening to music—you need to hear bikes, cars, or unexpected "G'day!"s from passing joggers.
- **Let someone know where you're going** if it's a long or new route, or even send a quick text "off for a walk/jog back in 30" that way someone knows where you're better to sound dramatic then go missing like a sock in the wash.
- **Where bright or reflective clothing** even during the day, a little neon or reflective strip can make you more visible at night .
- **Carry your phone, ID and a bit of cash**, your phone isn't just for selfies mid jog it is your safety net. Keep it charged, bring ID, and a few coins or a card in case you need water or a ride home.
- **Trust your gut always!** if someone gives you the eck, a car slows down weirdly, or a street feels off listen to that gut feeling turnaround, cross the road, or duck into a shop. You don't owe anyone politeness at the cost of your safety.
- **Mix up your routine** don't walk or jog the exact same route, at the exact same time ,every day. It sounds paranoid but it makes it harder for someone to track your habits.
- **Carry a personal safety device** if it helps you feel better this could be a whistle, a personal alarm, a smart watch with an emergency SOS feature.

- **Warming up and cooling down**, hydrate yes this is about physical safety to stretch before and after drink water avoid starting like a rocket and ending up like a broken wheelbarrow
- **Be smart**, walk or jog facing traffic so you can see what's coming, use pedestrian crossings, don't assume drivers see you make eye contact at intersections if you can

Gym Safety because we want gains not sprains.

- **Warm- up** before you go full Hulk don't skip the warm-up, your muscles need a gentle "hello" before you start pushing them 5 to 10 minutes on the treadmill, bike, or rowing machine, gentle stretches to get blood flowing, focus on the areas your training that day, cold muscle equals pulled muscles and we don't want that.
- **Wipe down equipment** (no one wants to share your sweat), and we don't want to catch their germs.
- **Don't hog equipment** or be a drop zone diva take turns, put weights back yes, even the heavy ones don't drop dumbbells from shoulder height like Thors hammer gym etiquette equals gym safety.
- **Listen to your body** if something hurts in a sharp weird way. Dizziness, nausea, sit down and breathe feeling shaky or light-headed, it's not just pushing through. It's a red flag rest, recover, and come back stronger.
- **Cool down** like you mean it stretch, breathe, walk it off, a proper cool-down helps reduce soreness, stiffness, and injury. It also gives you one moment to appreciate how strong you're becoming.
- **Don't forget hygiene,** bring a towel share if you're heading somewhere after wash your hands after using equipment especially before eating gym floors, change rooms, and mats equal bacteria playground if you're not careful.

- **Know your limit** and celebrate your wins you're not here to complete with six pack poses next to you. You're there to feel good, build strength, and care for your body. Push yourself sure but don't break yourself doing it.
- **Remember** if you're not sure ask a trainer if you feel unsafe let the staff know and at first it's always a good idea to go to the gym through staff and hours.

Mental Health Matters

Stress Happens, So Learn to Manage It

- What is stress really stresses your body's natural response to pressure, a little can help you get things done, too much, it messes with your sleep, mood, body, memory, immune system and even your gut. Stress isn't weakness, it's your brain's way of saying, I'm juggling too much, and one more thing Will send me over the edge.

Some And Sign Your Stress Even If You Think You're Fine

- Headaches or jaw clenching
- Snapping at people even when you don't mean to
- Forgetfulness
- Racing hard or short breath
- Tight shoulders or stomach pain
- Trouble sleeping or waking up exhausted
- Feeling overwhelmed by Tiny things
- The urge to run away from everything or hide under the doona

What Helps Stress? (besides screaming into a pillow)

- Breathe like you mean it slow, deep breath telling your nervous system we're safe. Try this inhale for four, hold for four, exhale for six do it for one minute you'll feel the difference.

Move Your Body

- No you don't need to hit the gym for an hour. Just move stretch, walk, dance to one song in your kitchen movement releases tension and reset your mood.

Social Media Detox

- If scrolling leaves you feeling like everyone's living their best life except you, take a break. Social media isn't real life—it's everyone's highlight reel.

Get It Out Of Your Head

- stress multiplies when it stays trapped in your mind write it down, say it out loud, voice note to a friend, cry if you need to your brain needs a release valve.

Eat, Sleep, Water, Repeat

- I know it sounds simple, but it's your foundation, eat something nourishing, drink a glass of water, get a proper night sleep or a nap, rest without guilt your body handle stress better when it's not running on fumes and crumbs.

Journelling

- Generally it's not just for poets, Overthinkers, or people who buy fancy notebooks. Journalling is simply writing down what's in your head so you can stop worrying about it all day long it helps you to process emotions, untangled thoughts, spot patterns in your behaviour, calm anxiety, boost clarity, confidence, and creativity best of all there are no rules.
- White works well when you write something down, your brain stops treating it like an emergency. It says someone's got it handled and chills out a bit journalling. Also give your perspective you can step back and say wow I'm dealing with a lot and I'm doing better than I thought.

Types Of Journelling

- brain get everything out, messy, real, unfilled like no one's ever going to read it because they won't
- Gratitude log write three things you're thankful for each day big or small overtime, this rewires your brain to look for the good stuff on even the messiest days
- Feeling trucker each morning or night jot down.... how do I feel? Why might i feel this way? What do I need right now? Simple powerful grounding.
- Prompts to explore feeling stuck? Try these "right now. I need..." "Something that's been weighing on me is... ""I'm proud of myself for..." "I want to go off... " "If I weren't scared I would...".
- Manifestation and goal city right like it's already happening I am building a calm, strong life. I am safe to speak. I am becoming the version of me. I used to dream about.

How To Start Journelling

- Grab any notebook or use your phone if that's easier.
- Set a timer for 5 to 10 minutes.
- Without editing.
- No grammar, no spelling checks, no pressure.
- Just honesty, scribbles, dot point ,swear word if needed.
- Just write...

Know When to Get Help

- Feeling off for more than a few days? Talk to someone. Beyond Blue, Headspace, or your GP—they're all there to help
- When you're constantly feeling overwhelmed if your brain feels like it's has 74 tabs open and everything feels too much ask for help.
- When you're scared of your own thoughts if you're having thought of harming yourself, feeling like you you can't go on, or question your words stop everything and ask for help now. Call someone call the helpline go to a doctor you deserve to live, heal, and be supported through this always.
- **Mum Tip**: There's no shame in needing support. Even superheroes need sidekicks.

Important Aussie Helplines And Support

- Lifeline - 13 11 14 24/7 crisis support
- Beyond Blue - 1300 224 636 mental health support
- Kids helpline - 1800 551 800 for ages 5 to 25
- Suicide callback service - 1300 659 467

Doctor, Dentist, and the Dreaded Check-Ups

Regular GP Visits

- Don't wait until you're half-dead to see a doctor, get a check-up once a year, even if you feel fine, yes obvious i know.

Dentist Drama

- Yes, dental visits are expensive, but they're cheaper than fixing a cavity or dealing with a toothache at 3 a.m. Brush, floss, and see your dentist at least once a year.
- **Mum Wisdom**: If you don't floss, you're just brushing 70% of your teeth.

Sexual Health

If you're sexually active, get tested regularly. It's quick, easy, and no one will judge you—least of all your doctor.

When Should You Get Tested

- up to unprotected sex
- If you have a new partner
- If your partner has other partners
- If you notice any unusual symptoms discharge, etc
- Once a year as a routine check up even if you feel fine

Where Can you Get Tested

- your local GP Dr book a standard appointment say you want an "STI screening" or a "sexual health check" it's normal, GPs do this all the time.

- Sexual health clinics free or low cost they are confidential non-judgy, seriously they've seen and heard it all. Find one via the Health Direct Clinic Finder.
- Family planning clinics great for all ages of testing, contraception, advice, and Info on safe sex.
- University of youth health services if you're under 25 or a student ask your student health Center.

Aussie Health Essentials

Sunscreen Is Non-Negotiable

- Slip, slop, slap. The Aussie sun doesn't mess around. Use SPF 30+ and reapply if you're outside for more than two hours.
- **Mum Wisdom**: Yes, even if it's cloudy. Sunburn isn't a good look on anyone.

Bug Repellent Is Your Best Mate

- Mozzies love fresh blood. Protect yourself with bug spray, especially in summer.

First Aid Kit

- Every home needs one. Stock it with:
- Band-aids
- Antiseptic cream
- Painkillers
- Tweezers
- A thermometer
- Sterile gauze pads
- Adhesive tape

- Antiseptic wipes
- Saline solution for cleaning wounds or eyes
- Scissors
- Disposable gloves
- Crêpe bandage for wrapping
- Instant cold pack
- Triangular bandage can be used as a sling
- Panadol or Nurofen
- Antihistamines
- Electrolytes
- Heat pack ideally instant
- CPR Face shield
- Emergency blanket foil thermal blanket
- First aid manual or instruction card
- Notepad and pen to record vitals or notes for paramedics
- Emergency contact numbers including poison Info 131126

Mum's Extra Aussie Health Tips

Sunscreen Is Life

- Slip, slop, slap every day—yes, even in winter. The Aussie sun doesn't take holidays

Bug Spray and Mozzie Nets

- If you're heading into mozzie territory (anywhere near water in summer), protect yourself. Dengue fever and itchy bites aren't fun.

Hydration Is Key

- Heatwaves can sneak up on you. Drink more water, especially if you're outside or exercising.
- **Mum Tip**: Coconut water or electrolyte tablets can help if you're feeling wiped out.

Mum's Quick Health Hacks

1. Feeling Dizzy

- Sit down, put your head between your knees, and sip water slowly if available suck on chocolate or lollies for the sugar it can help raise your blood pressure again.

2. Caught a Cold

- Rest, stay hydrated, and take paracetamol if you need it.
- Colds are annoying but harmless.
- Drink warm lemon water with honey
- Herbal teas such as peppermint, chamomile, ginger.
- Broth or chicken soup.
- Lozenges are great for sore throats or sprays.
- Over the counter helpers but make sure to speak to the the chemist first.

Sore Muscles

- A warm bath with Epsom salts works wonders. Bonus: it's like a mini spa day at home.

Blisters

- Cover them with a padded Band-Aid and avoid popping them—they're your body's natural bandage.

Feeling Tired All the Time?

- Check your iron levels—it's common in young adults, especially if you don't eat much red meat.

Hungover?

- Drink water, Electrolytes, Coconut water, Ginger Tea, Fresh Juice, Bone broth
- Eat something salty.
- Nap. No, the hair of the dog won't help.

Why You've Got This

Staying healthy isn't about being perfect—it's about looking after yourself so you can enjoy life to the fullest.
With a few good habits, regular check-ups, and maybe an extra glass of water here and there, you'll feel your best and be ready for whatever adventures come your way.

Love, Mum

Fever – When to Worry

What even is a fever?

A fever is when your body tem hits 38"C or higher. It's your body's way of saying, "Oi! Something's not right. I'm fighting it off.

Call the doctor or head to hospital if:

1. **The fever hits 39.5"C or higher**
2. **It doesn't go down with paracetamol or ibuprofen**
3. **It lasts more than 2-3 days**
4. **You're getting worse, not better** I if you confusion, rash, neck stiffness, chest pain, shortness of breath, or vomiting
5. **You're freezing and sweating at the same time**
6. **You've got other health issues** --weakened immune, asthma, diabetes, or a history of health complications
7. **You're feeling faint, weak, or out of it**

> **Mum's Thermometer Test:**
> *If you take your temp and say, 'Oof.,. that's a bit high,"*
> *and you also feel like you've been hit by a bus—*
> *don't wait. Make the call.*

Who to contact (Australia):

Nurse-on-Call (VIC): **1300 60 60 24**

Healthdirect (AUS-wide): **1800 022 222**

000 If someone is unresponsive, can't breathe properly, or is deteriorating fast

9

Adulting On The Move

Why Knowing Your Car Basics Is a Big Deal

Owning a car is a bit like having a very needy pet. It needs regular feeding (petrol), grooming (washing), and the occasional trip to the vet (mechanic). But unlike a goldfish, if you don't look after it, it won't just float—it'll leave you stranded on the side of the road. Mum's here to make sure you know your car stuff so you can avoid unnecessary drama and keep cruising smoothly.

Step 1: The Bare Minimum Every Driver Should Know

Please refer back to chapter 4 for a detailed explanation on how to change a tyre and jumpstart your battery!

How to Check Your Oil

- Why It's Important: Your car's engine needs oil like you need coffee—it doesn't run well without it.

How to Do It:

- Open the bonnet (it's the lever under the dashboard—check your manual if you're lost).
- Pull out the dipstick, wipe it clean, and stick it back in.
- Pull it out again and check the oil level. If it's low, top it up with the right oil (your manual knows the type)

Please note not all models have this option available for the dip stick please refer to your manual or make a quick call to the local mechanic to shop you yes you may need to speak to someone.

Changing a Tyre

- Why It's Important: Tyres don't care where you're going on how late you are—they'll go flat whenever they feel like it.
- Pull over somewhere safe and turn on your hazard lights.
- Loosen the lug nuts (turn anti-clockwise) before jacking up the car.
- Look underneath near the flat tire find the small indented or re-inforced area. That's your point for jacking the car up.
- Line up the jack so it's stable and squarely under that point

- Slowly raise the car until the tire is just off the ground
- Swap the tyre, tighten the nuts, and lower the car.
- Don't forget to re-tighten once it's on the ground!

How To Know Where To Put The Jack

- where does the Jack go on a car ? jacking it up in the wrong spot. Is a very bad day.
- The short answer you placed the jack under the cars jacking point a reinforced bit of metal designed just for this. It's usually just behind the front wheel or just in front of the rear wheel depending on which tire you're changing.
- Look for a small notch or groove underneath the car near each wheel.
- Sometimes a sticker or diagram on the inside of the drivers door or in your car manual is available.
- It might even be slightly raised have a flat metal plate to rest the jack on.

Never Jack Under

- The floor pen, it'll bend.
- The door sill your crush it.
- Random part of the suspension, you'll regret it.
- **Never** put your body under the car ever when it's on a jack **ever, ever, ever.**
- Use your spare only as a temporary fix, get the original tire fixed or replaced ASAP.
- Put something like a brick or a wedge, if possible behind the opposite tire so the car doesn't roll.
- Always remember to turn on your hazard lights.

Every Car is different if you can check the cars manual and

remember it its ok to ask for help.

What's in Your Tyres?

- Air. They Need Air.
- Check your tyre pressure monthly at a servo, too low, and you're burning more fuel; too high, and they're a bit dangerous. Your car's manual or the sticker on the driver's door should tell you the correct pressure.
- Park close to the air pump, pull up so the hose can comfortably reach all four tyres.
- Turn off the engine and apply the handbrake, safety first always.
- As mentioned above, find your recommended tire pressure for your car it'll say something like front 32 PSI rear 30 PSI.
- Remove the valve cover, that's a little black cap on your tyres black valve, keep it somewhere safe you will lose otherwise.
- Set the air pump to your target pressure pumps have a digital screen use the button to set it to your tyres PSI
- Attach the air hose nozzle to the valve push the nozzle on firmly you'll hear a little hiss sound hold it there. Pump will beep when the pressure is reached and stop automatically.
- Check the reading if the pump doesn't beep automatically some show a live reading top it up slowly until it hits the right number, these pumps are rare but may exist.
- Repeat for all tyres, yes or four and if you've got a spare tire and it's accessible check that one too.
- Replace the valve cups screw them back on don't leave your valves exposed to dirt or moisture.

Extra Tip From Mum

- Do it on cold tyres first thing in the morning is best he makes air band and messes with the reading.

- Check your pressure every 2 to 4 weeks, especially for long drive or road trips.
- If your tire keeps losing air, get it checked for slow leak or puncture.
- Low tire pressure equals bad fuel economy, uneven tire and unset hand so don't ignore it.

How to Jump-Start a Car
Why It's Important: Batteries die at the worst times.
Knowing this trick will save you a lot of waiting
(and money). Yes we touched on this before!

Mum's Instructions:

- Grab jumper cables.
- Connect red to red (positive terminals) and black to black (negative terminals).
- Start the working car, then yours. Let it run for a few minutes before disconnecting the cables (reverse order).
- Drive around for 30 minutes or sit there to recharge the battery.
  DON'T TURN THE CAR OFF

Maintenance = Fewer Headaches Later

Regular Servicing

- **Why It's Important**: Skipping services might save you money now, but it'll cost you way more in the long run.
- **Mum Tip**: Book your car in for a service every 10,000 km or once a year—whichever comes first.

Windscreen Wipers

- If they're squeaking or leaving streaks, replace them. Good visibility is non-negotiable, these can be purchased for your car at places like Super Cheap Auto and Repco these places often have a service available that they will install them for you, but honestly they are not hard to replace yourself you don't need to see a mechanic.

Petrol Doesn't Grow on Trees

- Before fueling up look at your fuel light you will see a little arrow that may look like s triangle on its side, this is the indicator of what side your fuel cap is.
- When opening your fuel cap, check the little sticker on the inside of the fuel door, it will tell you the fuel you can use always check this... get it wrong and put diesel in a petrol car and we have a big problem.
- Always keep your tank at least a quarter full—it's good for the car, your car fuel pump sits inside the tank and it uses petrol to cool and lubricate itself. When you run low fuel the pump can overheat and wear out faster, replacing it is not cheap.
- Over time, dirt and grime settle in your tank, when you run near empty, your fuel system may suck up the gunk clogging your fuel filters or even do damaging to your engine.
- You could run out at any moment, sometimes that could be the worst possible moment, in peak hour traffic, on a freeway, in the middle of nowhere, at night in the rain with no phone reception you get the picture let's not risk it.
- A little thing to remember your fuel gauge isn't perfect that 20 km left reading. It's an estimate and hills, traffic, Aircon, or driving faster can drain it quicker than expected. Suddenly you're comfy buffer is gone and you're coasting on prayers.

Keep It Clean

- Inside and out. A clean car runs better. Okay, that's not scientifically proven, but it's true in your heart.

Emergency Kit for Your Car

Every car needs a basic kit for the "just in case" moments:

- **Jumper Leads**: For when your battery decides to nap.
- **Spare Tyre and Tools**: Tyre jack, lug wrench, and gloves (because grease isn't a good look).
- **Torch**: With batteries (or a rechargeable one).
- **First Aid Kit**: Because you can't put a Band-Aid on a broken car, but you can on yourself.
- **Blanket and Water**: In case you're stuck waiting for help.
- **Phone Charger**: Your lifeline to call roadside assistance.
- **Duct Tape**: Fixes nearly everything.

Mum's Driving Tips

Always Check Your Mirrors

- Before reversing, pulling out, or even sneezing—check your surroundings.

Don't Drive Distracted

- That text can wait. Hands on the wheel, eyes on the road, that drink bottle you dropped on the back seat? leave it until its safe to pull over safely and grab it then.

Take Care of Your Tyres

- Rotate them every 10,000 km and replace them when the tread's low (stick a 20c coin in the grooves; if the edges of the coin are visible, it's time for new tyres).

Roadside Assistance Is Worth It

- Invest in NRMA or RACQ membership. It's like having a car-savvy mate on speed dial.

Aussie Road Rules Mum Wants You to Know

- **Indicate Early**: Your blinker isn't a surprise party—use it well in advance.
- **Keep Left Unless Overtaking**: Yes, even on quiet highways.
- **Don't Tailgate**: You're not a mozzie, so don't hover so close to the car in front.
- **Watch for Wildlife**: Kangaroos don't look both ways. Drive cautiously, especially at dawn and dusk.

When to Call for Help

1.The Engine Light Is On

- If it's glowing, book a service soon. If it's flashing, pull over and call a mechanic ASAP.

2. Flat Battery but No Jumper Leads?

- Call roadside assistance or a mobile mechanic—they're life-savers.

3. Accident on the Road?

- Stay calm. Check for injuries, call **000** if necessary, and exchange details with the other driver. Take photos for insurance (yes, even if it's just a tiny scratch).

Why You've Got This
Cars might seem complicated, but with a bit of knowledge and a few tools, you'll handle them like a pro. Whether it's a flat tyre, a dead battery, or just figuring out which side the petrol cap's on (hint: it's on the same side as the arrow on your dashboard), you've got this. And remember, if all else fails, call roadside assistance..

Love, Mum

10

Why Public Transport Isn't As Scary As It Looks

Public transport is like that one unreliable mate—you know it's going to show up eventually, but it might be late, and it'll probably come with baggage. But here's the thing: it's also cheap, convenient, and way better for your wallet than petrol prices. With some know-how, a solid survival kit, and a sense of humour, you'll soon be navigating the chaos like the seasoned commuter you're destined to be.

The Basics of Public Transport

1. Get Your Card Sorted

- **Opal, Myki, or Go Card?** Every Aussie state has its own magical plastic card that lets you ride. Treat it like gold because without it, you're either stranded or begging for change.
- **Mum Tip**: Always top it up. No one wants to be *that person* holding up the line at the station while frantically googling "how to top up Myki."

2. Know Your Timetable

- Download your local transport app (like TripView or TransLink) so you can keep track of buses, trains, and the occasional tram. Trust me, the one time you don't check is the day your bus decides to skip your stop.
- **Mum Wisdom**: Always allow an extra 15 minutes. Public transport runs on its own mysterious schedule, not yours.

3. Learn Your Routes

- If you're heading somewhere new, do a test run first. This is especially true if it involves more than one bus—nobody wants to be that lost-looking person at the interchange.
- **Mum Tip**: Take note of landmarks. You'll feel like Dora the Explorer, but at least you won't miss your stop.

Public Transport Etiquette (How Not to Be "That Person")

1. Don't Hog the Priority Seats

- If you're young, fit, and not holding a baby, move. That's not your throne.

2. Keep Your Music to Yourself

- Your playlist might be a banger, but I promise you, no one else wants to hear it. Get headphones—and use them wisely.

3. Move Down the Aisle

- Blocking the door is not a personality trait. Move in, let others on, and remember: we're all just trying to survive this commute.

4. Take Your Rubbish With You

- Public transport isn't a bin, and your half-eaten kebab is no one else's responsibility.

Survival Kit for Public Transport

Every commuter needs a few essentials for surviving the journey—and maybe even enjoying it:

- **Reusable Water Bottle**: Hydration is the difference between "fresh-faced commuter" and "zombie with a Myki."
- **Headphones**: For drowning out the awkward silence or the guy loudly explaining cryptocurrency on his phone.

- **Snacks**: A muesli bar can turn a delayed train into a bearable experience. Pro tip: avoid loud snacks—no one likes a cruncher.
- **Book or E-Reader**: Look intellectual *and* avoid eye contact. Double win.
- **Power Bank**: Because your phone dying halfway through a delay is just cruel.
- **Hand Sanitiser**: Public transport poles are basically germ factories.
- **Tissues**: For sneezes, spills, and the occasional tear when you realise you're on the wrong bus.
- **Tote Bag**: For impromptu shopping or lugging home free community newspapers you didn't want but couldn't say no to.

Safety on Public Transport

1. Stick to Well-Lit Stops and Stations

- If you're commuting at night, stick to busy, well-lit areas while waiting for your ride.

2. Keep Your Valuables Secure

- Use a bag that zips up and keep it in front of you, especially in crowded spaces. Pickpockets love an easy target.
- **Mum Tip**: If you can't feel your wallet, it's in the wrong spot.

3. Trust Your Gut

- If someone's giving you bad vibes, move to another carriage or sit near the driver.

4. Avoid Empty Carriages at Night

- Stick to the busier ones—it's safer, and you won't feel like the star of a low-budget horror movie.

5. Stay Alert

- Keep one ear free if you're using headphones, and don't get too engrossed in your phone. Being aware of your surroundings is your best defence.

Handling Public Transport Curveballs

1. Delays

- Check the app, stay calm, and let whoever's waiting know you're running late.
- **Mum Tip**: Always carry snacks. Delayed trains are way less painful with a Tim Tam in hand.

2. Lost Property

- Left your jacket on the train? Contact the transport authority ASAP. Don't wait a week and then wonder why no one's kept your umbrella for you.

3. Missed Stops

- Get off at the next stop and regroup. No one's judging you (except maybe yourself).

4. Dodgy Encounters

- Move to a busier section or tell the driver. Weirdos are no match for a quick-thinking commuter.
- **Mum Wisdom**: Trust your instincts. If something feels off, it probably is.

Mum's Extra Public Transport Safety Tips

1. **Share Your Location**: If you're travelling late, let a friend or family member know where you are. Most phones let you share your live location.
2. **Emergency Contacts**: Have your emergency contact saved in your phone under ICE ("In Case of Emergency").
3. **Carry Cash or a Card**: Always have a backup for unexpected expenses or if your transport card runs out.
4. **Know Your Exits**: Whether it's the bus, train, or tram, always clock the nearest exit in case you need to get off quickly.

Why You've Got This
Public transport might not be glamorous, but with a little planning, a solid survival kit, and a focus on safety, you'll master it in no time. Whether you're navigating rush hour or the midnight express, remember:confidence is key, snacks are crucial, and Mum's wisdom is always with you.

Love, Mum

11

Why Talking To People Feels Weird

Ever walk into a conversation and immediately want to backpedal out like a cartoon character? Don't worry, you're not alone. Most people are just winging it, hoping they sound halfway intelligent. The good news? You don't need to be a TED Talk champion to hold a decent convo. With a few tricks, a dash of humour, and some Mum-approved tips, you'll be chatting like a pro faster than a seagull snatches chips at the beach.

The Mum-Approved Confidence Cheats

1. Stand Like You're the Boss (Even If You're Not)

- Shoulders back, chin up, feet planted like you've just been handed the keys to the city. Good posture says, "I know what I'm doing," even if your brain's screaming, "What's happening!?"
- **Mum Tip:** Practice at home. Channel your inner Beyoncé—she didn't conquer the world slouching.

2. Speak Slowly
(But Not Like You're Narrating a Nature Documentary)

- Mum Wisdom: If you speak too fast, you'll sound like a horse race commentator. Too slow, and people might wonder if you're buffering. Aim for calm and steady, like a soothing GPS voice.

3. Eye Contact (But Don't Go Full Serial Killer)

- Looking people in the eye shows confidence, but don't overdo it—there's a fine line between "engaged" and "staring into their soul." If it's awkward, focus on their nose. They'll never know.

4. Smile Like You Mean It (But Don't Overdo It)

- A natural smile says, "Hey, I'm approachable!" A forced, toothy grin says, "I might sell essential oils." Keep it chill.

Starting a Conversation Without Sounding Like a Robot

1. The Magic Word: "Hi"

- It's simple, effective, and not at all weird. Follow it with something relevant, like, "This event is great, isn't it?" or, "I can't believe we're queuing this long for coffee."

2. Compliments Work Every Time

- "That jacket is amazing!" or, "Your haircut is next level!" are icebreakers that never fail. Bonus: people love talking about themselves, so you're giving them a chance to shine.

3. Open-Ended Questions Are Your Best Friend

- Avoid the yes/no traps. Instead of, "Did you enjoy the movie?" try, "What did you think of that plot twist?" If all else fails, ask about their pets. Everyone loves talking about their fur babies.

How to Sound Like a Total Pro (Even When You're Winging It)

1. Stay Curious

- Don't know much about what they're talking about? Perfect. Ask questions. "Oh, you're into kayaking? What's that like?" makes you look interested, not clueless.

2. Have a Go-To Topic

- Keep a few safe topics in your back pocket:
- **Food**: "Know any good spots around here?"

- **TV**: "Seen anything binge-worthy lately?"
- **Travel**: "If you could book a flight right now, where would you go?"
- **Mum Tip**: Avoid pineapple-on-pizza debates. They get heated fast.

3. Avoid the Big No-Nos

- Politics, religion, and "Why do people post gym selfies?" are conversational minefields. Skip them unless you're ready for a debate.

Surviving Awkward Moments Like a Legend

1. Forget Their Name? Don't Panic

- Mum's Trick: "Wait, how do you spell your name again?" Works like a charm, unless their name is Bob.

2. When the Conversation Hits a Wall

- "So, what's been keeping you busy lately?" is your conversational lifesaver. It's broad enough for them to run with, and it makes you sound genuinely interested.

3. Laugh It Off

- Said something weird? Stumbled over your words? Own it. A quick, "Well, that was awkward—let's pretend that didn't happen!" works every time.

Wrapping It Up Without Being Weird

1. The Polite Exit

- "It's been great chatting, but I'd better mingle!" or "I'll let you get back to it—catch you later!" says, "I'm leaving," without being abrupt.

2. Leave a Positive Note

- A quick compliment or a "Thanks for the chat!" makes sure you're remembered as a legend, not "that person who bolted mid-sentence."

Mum's Golden Rules for Talking to Anyone

1. **Practice Everywhere**: Chat to the barista, your Uber driver, or the neighbour whose name you still don't know. It's like training wheels for big conversations.
2. **Keep It Light**: Not every chat needs to be profound. A simple, "How good is this weather?" can work wonders.
3. **Remember, Everyone's Awkward Sometimes**: Even the smooth talkers have their cringe moments. You're human—it's part of the charm.

Why You've Got This

Conversations don't have to be terrifying. With a little curiosity, a few tricks, and a smile that doesn't say, "Help me," you'll master the art of talking to people in no time. And remember: if all else fails, talk about their dog. Dogs make everything better.

Love, Mum

12

How To Handle Conflict

Conflict is like dropping a meat pie on your white shirt—unexpected, annoying, and hard to ignore. But here's the thing: learning to handle it is a life skill. Whether it's dealing with your housemate's questionable cleaning habits, your mate's "borrow and forget" tendencies, or a stranger who's just plain wrong, you can tackle any disagreement without turning it into a full-blown episode of Home and Away. Mum's here to teach you the ropes, with a side of laughs.

The Golden Rules of Conflict (Mum's Version)

1. Stay Calm (Or Fake It Like a Pro)

- creaming might feel good, but it also makes you look like you've been possessed by a magpie. Take a deep breath, count to five, and channel your inner yoga guru.
- **Mum Tip**: If staying calm isn't working, picture them trying to parallel park. Instant serenity.

2. Listen Like You Mean It

- Let them talk first—it's like letting someone else go through a spiderweb for you. You'll come out better on the other side.
- **Mum Wisdom**: Listening doesn't mean agreeing; it means you're not planning your comeback before they've even finished their sentence.

3. Stick to the Issue

- Keep the convo focused. This isn't your chance to remind them about that time they ate your leftover lasagna six months ago.

Talking It Out Without Making It a Dumpster Fire

1. Use "I" Statements (Not "You're the Problem" Statements)

- Bad: "You're the worst housemate ever for eating my Vegemite!"

- Good: "I feel frustrated when I buy Vegemite, and it disappears overnight."
- **Mum Tip**: People are less defensive when you talk about how *you* feel instead of accusing them of being the Vegemite bandit.

2. Watch Your Tone (Seriously, Watch It)

- Don't talk like you're auditioning for *Real Housewives of Australia.* A calm tone gets things done.
- **Mum Wisdom**: If your voice goes full banshee, expect them to go full wallaby in headlights.

3. Acknowledge Their Side (Even If They're Bonkers)

- "I get that you didn't mean to leave your socks everywhere, but it's driving me bananas" sounds better than "Your socks are the reason I'm losing my mind."

Handling Specific Types of Conflict (Because Every Drama Is Unique)

1. Housemate Shenanigans

- **The Problem**: Dishes in the sink, noise at midnight, or mystery hair in the shower.
- **The Fix**: Call a house meeting. Set clear rules. If they can't handle it, there's always Gumtree for finding a new housemate.
- **Mum Tip**: A chore roster is like a contract—once it's on the fridge, it's law.

2. Workplace Nonsense

- **The Problem**: Office fridge thieves or "that guy" who takes credit for your ideas.
- **The Fix**: Be direct but polite. "Hey, I noticed you borrowed my idea in the meeting—let's work on it together next time" is firm but not spicy.
- **Mum Wisdom**: Always have receipts (metaphorically or literally). Evidence is your best mate.

3. Mate Missteps

- **The Problem**: Late-night cancellations or "borrowing" things permanently.
- **The Fix**: Be upfront. "Hey, I need my charger back—my phone's dying faster than a plant I forgot to water" works wonders.
- **Mum Tip**: If they can't respect you after a good chat, you might need to Marie Kondo that friendship.

Knowing When to Throw in the Towel (Or the Tea Towel)

1. Spot the Red Flags

- If they keep yelling, guilting, or refusing to hear you out, it might be time to walk away.
- **Mum Wisdom**: Sometimes it's not about winning—it's about not wasting your energy.

2. Agree to Disagree

- Not every disagreement needs a resolution. It's okay to part ways with a simple, "We see this differently, but that's fine."

3. Protect Your Sanity

- If the drama's taking over your life, it's time to step back. No one's got time for toxic nonsense.

Mum's Bonus Tips for Conflict Champions

1. Text First (If You're Raging)

- A quick, "Hey, can we chat about X later?" gives you time to chill before diving in.

2. Don't Over-Vent

- Telling everyone about your argument might feel good, but it can also blow up in your face. Stick to one trusted confidant.

3. Use a "Pause" Button

- Mid-argument? Say, "Let's take a break and come back to this." It's not weakness—it's strategy.

Why You've Got This

Handling conflicts isn't about being the loudest or the smartest it's about staying calm,being kind, and knowing when to stand your ground. With a little practice and a lot of patience, you can handle anything life throws at you, from stolen chips to coworkers chaos.

Love, Mum

13

Building Your Network
Trust me

Networking sounds like a kind of thing that involves awkward hand-shakes free bad coffee and those weird little nametags that don't stick properly but he's the truth. Building worker is just a fancy wave saying make some mates who have your back. It's not about business cards. It's about finding people who will help you grow whether it's landing a job finding a cheap flat or learning where to go the burst meat pies in town

Step one start with mates you've already got

Your friends are your OG network.

- Look around your mates your siblings even your neighbour's who wants to lend you a ladder. These people are part of your network. They may not be LinkedIn famous but they know people who know people.
- Uni groups clubs and that one bloke at the gym mention that what you're up to whether it's looking for a job plumbing planning a trip or hunting for a bargain you'll be amazed at who knows a guy who knows a guy who knows a guy.
- **Mum Tip** never underestimate the power of chatting with someone over sausage at Bunnings connections are everywhere.

Making new connections without being creepy

Lead with curiosity

- Networking isn't speed dating for jobs. It's about building relationships asking questions listening and then the chat flows naturally.
- **Mum Tip** think of it like making a new friend just keep the watch your star sign unless you're really relevant

Start with the basics

What do you do? Might seem basic but it's a gateway to deeper chat follow up.

- What do you love about it?
- Or how did you get into that?
- Don't overthink it people aren't sitting there judging you every word they're too busy worrying about what they are saying. Relax you're already smashing it just by showing up.

Finding mentors without feeling like a suck up

- **What's a mentor anyway?** A mentor is someone who's been where you're going and can help you navigate the potholes like a GPS but cooler.
- **How to spot a good one** look for someone who work you admire whether it's your boss or uni lecture or that one person on LinkedIn who post surprisingly helpful. Staff.
- **Ask without being awkward** start with polite messages I really admire your work. X would you have time for a quick coffee? I'd love to hear your advice.
- **Mum Tip** keep it short sweet nobody has time for messages longer than credits for neighbour's.

Keep your network alive so it doesn't go stale.

- Stay in touch, networking isn't a one and done deal. Check in with people, occasionally drop a message. Leave a comment or meet up for coffee.
- If you only reach out when you need something, you look like the one who made who only calls when they need to borrow your Ute.
- Share your wins got a new job smashed a project or finally figured out how to poach an egg share it with people , good people love seeing other succeeded, it makes them feel good too.
- Offer help even when you're busy, whether it's sharing a job listing or hyping up someone's work giving back keep your network strong.

Networking in the digital jungle

- LinkedIn isn't just for old people in suits, it's like the professional Facebook. Keep your profile up-to-date, share interesting stuff and connect with people you meet.
- **Mum tip** use the photo where you don't look like you've just woken up or been caught in a windstorm.
- Follow the right people from influencer's in your field to the people who always post from the best memes. Follow people who inspire you just don't slide into the DM's with "hey we're both in that same spreadsheet".
- Join online communities there's groups for everything. Find your niche and dive in to the discussion either on Facebook, Reddit or even a TikTok online connections are gold.

Mum's extra tips for networking like a pro

- Be nice manners matter a quick thanks for the chat or appreciate your advice goes a long way.
- Fake it till you make it feeling awkward confident confidence isn't about knowing everything is about not looking like you're about to bolt
- Don't forget to laugh networking can feel weird but it's just people talking to people if it's funny laugh if it's awkward laugh harder

Why you've got this?

Networking isn't about suits business cards or fake smiles. It's about building real relationships, helping others, letting them help you. In return whether meeting someone at a barbecue, online or over coffee the key is be yourself but the polite non-borrowing your mates Netflix password version.

Love Mum

14

Online Safety Stranger Danger

Alright love let's have a heart to heart about the wild West that is the Internet. I know it's whe loud voices and people pretending to be someone they're not so here's a few rules to keep your digital safe self as safe as your real one

YOUR PASSWORD SHOULDN'T BE PASSWORD 123

1. Yes I know it's easier to remember but it's also easier to hack than a microwave with no door make your password weird and unusable bonus points. If even you have to reset it every time you login.

Mum Tip - use a password manager it's like a tidy drawer for all your digital keys.

1. IF it seems too good to be true, it's probably dodgy, it's un-likely to be a mysterious Royal from Overseas it's going to send you $2 million for clicking a think I know you didn't win an iPhone you never entered a competition for. Cam is a clever but you're clever if it smells Off Bin it.
2. Don't over share, you wouldn't walk into a food court and shout your own full name birthdate and where you live your favourite sandwich and what school you went to so don't do it online either keep the mystery life scam is love a good Facebook stalk.
3. Turn onto factor authentication yes, annoying but so he's get-ting your account hacked and watching someone pretend to be you while selling fake Ray-Bans a quick code sent to your phone worth it.
4. Don't chat with creepy strangers even if it's flirty "hi beautiful" or someone pretending to be a Cousin you've never heard of just don't if someone gives you the block and move on your safety is worth more than being polite.

5. Don't click weird links ever Got a message from your Bestie saying oh my god is this you in this video? Followed by suspicious link it's not them. It's a hacker. Text your mate directly and ask if they say what video you've dodged cyber bullet.

6. The Internet is not Your diary Once upon a time we used to write our thoughts in sparkly notebooks and heart-shaped padlocks. Now everyone's airing their business on TikTok sending screenshot or posting every breath on Instagram stories. Don't get me wrong. I'm not any social media but let's be clear. The Internet is forever.

So here's the extended version of our digital survival guide straight from your Mum who's seen more scams than a dodgy garage sale on Facebook marketplace

What you post stays posted

- Just because you deleted it doesn't mean it's gone, screenshots are faster than gossip in a group chat. Think before you post that rant, that risk a selfie, or that funny comment that could land you in hot water later. Future bosses google, so do nosy relatives if you wouldn't want your Grandma, your boss and your ex to all say it at once don't post it.... be social media savvy.
- Scammers are getting smarter and they love a trusting soul
- Don't click on random links
- Don't send money to anyone you haven't physically had coffee with
- Don't give your baking details, even if someone says your account at risk

- Don't fall for love bombs from people who look like models and leave 1000 km away
- **Mum Tip** - if someone says I'm stuck over season eight $200 for a flight home they're lying unless it's your actual Brother and even then ask for a selfie holding today's newspaper.

Your digital print is like glitter

- It out there it's everywhere employers landlord uni even potential dates will do a little dick. Keep a classy kind and maybe don't feel yourself doing a show unless you want it resurfacing in your wedding video.
- Watch out for catfish creeps - Not everyone online is who they say they are that funny flirty person with a profile full of quotes and travel pics could be a scammer or someone using a fake identity
- **Mum tip** - reverse image search profile pics and never meet someone in private for the first time public places broad daylight and texture location to someone first

Privacy settings are there for a reason

- Every app has them use them, set your Insta to private lock your Facebook profile approve tagged photos. You don't need your boss your ex or your nine maths teacher seeing what you got up to on Friday night.

Protect your mental health

- Social media can be a highlight reel and it's easy to start thinking someone's got it better than you remember no one post their breakdowns bad breath or bank account. Unfollow people will make you feel like rubbish meat block delete your piece is worth more than a double tap.

Stay informed not overwhelmed

- The Internet is full of opinions disguised as facts before you repost that shocking article or by into a panic field post check your sources. If it sounds sensational it probably is stick to reliable website and if something doesn't feel right deeper it's okay to ask questions in fact it's encouraged.

Its Ok to log off

- Real life doesn't happen behind the screen. It's happening right in front of you even if it's just a cup of tea and your cat staring at the wall like it's haunted.
- Take breaks touch grass laugh with friends in person and no you don't owe anyone online your time your energy or your attention
- **Mum wisdom** you're clever kind and capable but no one is scam proof and no one is immune to digital overload so keep your wits about you. Protect your peace and remember when in doubt call your mum or someone you can trust.

What to do if you feel unsafe online

- Let me be really clear here if something doesn't feel right it probably isn't your gut is your inner alarm bell trust it even if someone's making you feel uncomfortable threatening you or you stumbled across something that feels off he's exactly what to do.

- One stop engaging immediately.
- Don't reply don't argue don't explain.
- Block unfriend delete you're not obligated to be polite to someone who is making you feel unsafe.

To take screenshots

- Before you block or report anything take screenshot screenshots, messages, usernames profiles anything suspicious if things escalate you'll want a record of what is happening

Three reported it

- Every platform has a way to report abuse harassment, fake profiles or dangerous content. Use it. They're there for a reason and it help helps protect other people too.

Quick links

- Instagram reporting help
- Facebook safety Centre
- E safety commissioner Australia for serious online abuse image based on abuse or cyber bullying

Tell someone you trust

- This bit important if something or someone online is making you scared confused or uncomfortable tell someone a parent. I made a teacher a counsellor or even a mum. You're not overreacting you're not being a drama queen or king and you are not alone. This is a time to actually ask for help nobody is going to judge you.

If it's serious, call it in

- If someone is threatening you sharing private imagery or trying to meet you in person in a creepy or pushy way that is serious contact the police. You can also call crimestoppers on one 800 333000 or lifeline on 13 1114 if you're feeling emotionally overwhelmed

Protect your account accounts

- If you think someone's hacked you or tried to access your Info change your password straight away turn onto factor authentication log out of all devices
- Seven take a break and breathe
- Feeling scared online can shake you up it's okay to step back. Take a breath log off and give yourself. Space. Go for a walk. Talk it out with someone watch something that makes you laugh. Seinfeld is great for that.

Why you've got this?

The Internet is a brilliant tool, but it's not always a safe place. Be smart be cautious and if you're ever unsure ask someone you trust just remember if they're an oldie like me they've survived dial-up Internet and MSN Messenger. And remember you're never being too sensitive for feeling unsafe you're allowed to have boundaries and you are always allowed to ask for help no matter what there is always someone who has got your back even if all you need is someone to sit with you awhile to help you change your password and eat half a packet of Tim Tams.

WHAT TO DO IF YOU FEEL UNSAFE ONLINE

If something doesn't feel right, it probably isn't.

1. STOP ENGAGING IMMEDIATELY

Block, unfriend, delete. You're not an obligation to engage to someone ho is unsase.

2. TAKE SCREENSHOTS

Messages, usernames, profiles, anything supizious

3. REPORT IT

Use platform to report abuse abuse, harassment, fake profiles, or danger.

instagram Reporting Help · Facebook Safety Center
· eSafety Commissioner (Australia)

4. TELL SOMEONE YOU TRUST

Tell someone as parent, a mate teacher, or other.

5. IF IT'S SERIOUS~CALL IT IN

If antone hacked — if breats, or pushy or pushy. Crime Stoppers (Australia): 1800 333 000, Lifeline

6. PROTECT YOUR ACCOUNTS

Change your passwords and two factor authentication.

Love Mum Reminder. You are not alone. Help is always

15

Hiking Without Getting Eaten by a Drop Bear

There's nothing quite like hitting the Aussie bush breathing in the eucalyptus and air and feeling like bear Grylls minus the raw lizard breakfast but whether you're going on a Sunday stroll or a proper multi day trip track let's have a quick safety chat yea?

Because as as a mum, it's literally my job to imagine you stranded lost or being chased by a very ambitious kangaroo.

OK the real talk on hiking smart and the app that'll keep you safe found and full of trail snacks.

Before you hit the Trail

- Tell someone where you're going no, this isn't overprotective. It's common sense text a mate, your partner, mum or someone that you trust with the; name of the trail, when you're leaving, and when you're due back, if you don't check in someone will know to come looking and yes with snacks

Take more water than you think

- I'm not saying your a camel, however even on a mild day you will burn through your water faster than you expect don't rely on creeks either unless you enjoy a splash of bacteria with your hydration remember animals pee too.

Where the right gear

- Thongs are not hiking shoes **I repeat thongs are not hiking shoes** wear proper boots, take a hat, chuck on sunscreen and layer up the bush can go from 30° to where's my thermals in a few hours.

Apps that'll make you hike like a pro and not get lost like a numpty

All trails

- I must have maps track reviews distance difficulty levels. It's like the TripAdvisor for hikes. You can even download maps to use off-line essentially in the middle of nowhere.

iOS and android free with optional pro upgrades
Emergency plus

- This one's non-negotiable developed by Aussie emergency services. It shows your exact GPS location so if you do need help, you can tell them exactly where you are no more near a big rock type guesses.

iOS and android free
Gaia GPS

- Great for serious hikers and backcountry explorers loads of detailed maps and topography data bonus. You can record your route as you go which is handy for not walking in circles like a confused wombat.

iOS and android free versions available pro for off-line maps
BOM weather app

- If anyone knows when the sky is about to drop a bucket of sideways rain, it's the bureau of meteorology always check it before heading out.

iOS and android free
First aid by St John ambulance Australia

- Even if you're going for a light bushwalk knowing what to do in a snakebite situation or how to handle a twisted ankle is worth this Waiting this app gives you the simple step-by-step instructions.

iOS and android free

If you're lost or it's an emergency while hiking

- First things first don't panic. You might be scared cold tired or annoyed at yourself by keeping calm. Is the best thing you can do right now you're not silly and you're not alone. Help can find you but here's what you have to do while you wait.
- One stop breathing
- As soon as you realise you're lost in trouble stop moving
- Sit down, take a few deep breaths and center yourself
- Try to remember when you last knew exactly where you were
- Look around calmly don't want to further unless you're absolutely sure of the way

Call for help even with no reception

- 000 is the number to call for emergency help in Australia.
- Dial 112. This is the emergency number that will try to connect you to any available network not just your provider EVEN IF YOU DONT HAVE SERVICE.
- You can also use the emergency plus app it will show your exact GPS coordinates even without mobile signal which is gold for rescue crews.

Make yourself visible

- If you've called for help or send a message stay put unless it's unsafe to do so.
- Find an open area where a helicopter or rescue team could see you.
- Layout bright clothing or gear to create contrast with the bush.
- If it's dark/a torch or your phone light intermittently.
- Stay warm and dry.
- Use a jacket poncho or emergency blanket to keep warm.

- Shelter under a tree or Rockledge if it rains but avoid creek or gully that could flood.
- **Mum tip** always pack an emergency foil blanket in your day pack they weigh nothing but can save your life.

Don't drain your battery

- Your Phone is your lifeline so
- Turn on low-power mode
- Close all the other apps
- Avoid checking it every five minutes just keep it handy in case help. Call you back.

Make noise safely

- If you hear people or think help is now shout clearly at intervals
- Blow whistle if you've got one three blasts equals universal distress signal
- Avoid screaming constantly you can wear you out and make it harder to hear a reply

Don't try to tough it out alone

- Even if you're embarrassed or think it's not serious enough it is okay to call for help people get disorientated in the bush all the time. This is what our amazing emergency services are for.

Quick emergency contact Australia

- 000 police fire ambulance
- 112 if there's no reception
- SES state emergency services 132 500

- ePIRB/PLB if you're doing serious solo hiking consider carrying a personal location beacon PLB

Why you've got this?

The most important thing in your pack is in a snack a map or even your phone. It's your common sense and courage and I know you've got both stay calm be smart and remember I'd rather Call for help then try to be here. Nature is magical but she doesn't look around. A bit of prep can be the difference between a beautiful hike and a full-blown search party.

HIKING SAFETY CHECKLIST
– BEFORE YOU HIT THE TRAIL

☐ **Told someone where I'm going**
(Name of track, time I lett, when I expect to be báck)

☐ **Downloaded my trail map offline**
(AllTrails, Gaia GPS, or written notes – don't rely on reception!)

☐ **Checked the weather forecast**
(BOM App is your mate. No one likes a surprise thunderstorm)

☐ **Packed anough water**
(At least 2L per person foshort hikes, more if it's hot or remote)

☐ **Packed snacks (and maybe extra snacks)**
(You're not yourself when you're hangry on a hill)

☐ **Wearing proper shoes**
(Thongs are for the beach. Hiking boots = happy feet)

☐ **Sunscreen, hat, and insect repellent**
(The Aussie trifecta of not becoming a tried, Itchy mess)

☐ **First aid kit packed**
(Snake bandage, painkillers, plasters... and maybe some antihistamines)

☐ **Phone is fully charged (and on low battery mode)**
(Consider a power bank if you're going bush for a while)

☐ **Downloaded these apps:** • Gaia GPS
  • AllTrails • St John First Aid

☐ **Trusting my gut** **LOVE *MUM REMINDER*:**
If you wouldn't let yourmáte walk into the bush unprepared, don't do it to yourself. You're precious cargo. Hike safe, hike smart, and always take the damn snacks.

16

A Few Last Words From Mum

Well here we are at the end of the book, if you've made it this far you've officially survived my ramblings, my mum jokes and probably more than one story about cleaning with vinegar. Congratulations sweetheart, you're now equipped with enough life skills to conquer the world or at least keep your laundry from smelling like sweaty gym bags.

Life is messy, unpredictable and occasionally involves screaming at a burnt piece of toast but that's the beauty of it, you'll figure it out as you go, the important thing is to keep trying keep, learning, keep laughing especially at yourself, trust me it helps. Whether you're making your first budget scrubbing mystery stains or navigating the chaos of being an adult remember this you're doing great.

You won't get everything right the first time or the 10th time but that's okay no one does and when in doubt ask for help, now I know not everyone has a mum to call when life feels overwhelming so let me say this I'm proud of you even if we've never met.

I see the courage it takes to show up for yourself everyday particularly when life has not always been kind, and circumstances have maybe put you at a disadvantage, but to try to learn and to keep going even when it's tough.

The world is lucky to have you and I hope you know how you are never truly alone, take this book as a hug from me, a reminder that someone out there is cheering you on, believing in you, and hoping you know, just how amazing you are, you've got this my loves.

Thank you for letting me be a part of your journey, I hope this book made you smile, gave you a few handy tips, and reminded you, that you are stronger, smarter, and more capable than you realise. You are loved! now go out there and smash it.

Don't forget to take the chicken out of the freezer

Love always Mum.

17

Author Bio

About the Author: Tina Maree

Tina Maree is a writer, mother, and self-proclaimed expert in the fine art of "figuring life out as you go." With a knack for turning life's everyday chaos into laugh-out-loud lessons, or learning how to putty, sand and paint a wall, Tina has made it her mission to help young adults navigate the messy, hilarious, and occasionally overwhelming world of *adulting*.

The eldest sibling of eight—five brothers and two sisters—Tina grew up surrounded by noise, laughter, and the kind of life lessons that only come from wrangling a big family. At the heart of her upbringing was her beloved grandmother Jean, whose incredible generosity, love, and wisdom left a mark that continues to guide Tina's life and work, long after Jean's passing.

Drawing on those roots of family, love, and resilience, as well as years of experience as a mum to her two greatest creations, Isabella and Nicholas, also the author of *"The enchanted wanderer series"* Tina combines practical advice with a generous dose of Aussie humour. Whether it's mastering the slow cooker, balancing a budget, or figuring out how to remove mysterious laundry stains, Tina writes like she talks: real, relatable, and with just the right amount of sass.

Tina's work is a heartfelt love letter to young adults finding their way helpful guidance and the kind of support only a "mum voice" can provide. When she's not writing or cleaning endlessly, you'll likely find her shopping at Pillow Talk, perfecting a recipe, re-organising a cupboard, or reminding her kids (again) to put their clothes in the washing basket, not on the bathroom floor NEXT to the basket.

www.ingramcontent.com/pod-product-compliance
Lightning Source LLC
Chambersburg PA
CBHW041955090426

42811CB00013B/1499